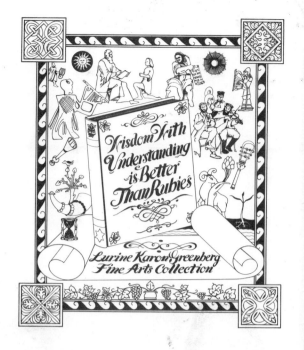

LONDON
IN OLD PHOTOGRAPHS
1897–1914

LONDON
IN OLD PHOTOGRAPHS
1897–1914

Felix Barker

Introduction by Alistair Cooke

A Bulfinch Press Book
Little, Brown and Company
Boston · New York · Toronto · London

farca

First North American Edition

ISBN 0-8212-2230-9
Library of Congress Catalog Card Number 95-76262

Bulfinch Press is an imprint and trademark of
Little, Brown and Company (Inc.)
Published simultaneously in Canada by
Little, Brown & Company (Canada) Limited
This book was produced by
Calmann & King Ltd., London

Designed by Karen Osborne
Picture research by Mary-Jane Gibson
Typeset by Bookworm Typesetting, Manchester

PRINTED IN SINGAPORE

FRONTISPIECE
London Bridge at the turn of the century.
Morning scene with City workers on their way
to their offices.

Contents

Acknowledgements *6*

Bibliography *6*

Chronology *7*

Introduction to an Age
by Alistair Cooke *9*

CHAPTER ONE
Victorian and Edwardian Photography *15*

CHAPTER TWO
London, Centre of the Empire *27*

CHAPTER THREE
Edward VII Makes Changes *43*

CHAPTER FOUR
The Growth of Edwardian London *77*

CHAPTER FIVE
Edwardians Enjoy Themselves *117*

CHAPTER SIX
Age of Unrest and Reform *161*

CHAPTER SEVEN
'Georgian' Epilogue *187*

Picture Credits *206*

Index *207*

Acknowledgements

Select Bibliography

A book ranging over so many events and illustrated by a large variety of contemporary photographs has needed a cross-fertilisation of ideas, and these have been generously provided by experts and friends. Among them I would like to name Frances Dimond, Curator of the Royal Photographic Archives at Windsor Castle, Terence Pepper, Curator of Photographs at the National Portrait Gallery, Kate Crowe in the Historical Branch of the Foreign and Commonwealth Office, Debbie Ireland at the Royal Photographic Society, the staff at the National Monument Record Office, and John Fisher and Jeremy Smith at the Guildhall Library. Richard Mangan, Curator of the Mander and Mitchenson Theatre Collection, Mrs A.S. Wheeler, Charterhouse School librarian, Beverley Williams, Assistant Curator at the Royal Engineers Museum, Chatham, Ken Kiss of the Crystal Palace Museum, Ron Spells, Director of James Russell and Sons, Wimbledon photographers. All have provided specialized information as have the archivists of local collections and many borough libraries.

As always I have had great help from my long-time friend and collaborator, Peter Jackson, on whose knowledge and famous private London Collection I have drawn; from Denise Silvester-Carr, who read the proofs and was constantly vigilant about royal matters; from John Richardson, Director of Historical Publications, who helped with the Chronology; and from my wife who carried out research and gave constant encouragement.

I have been fortunate in the extensive picture research of Mary-Jane Gibson; in assistance from the designer of the book, Karen Osborne, who generously extended her work to help me with the captions; and, above all, I am extremely grateful for advice, especially at the planning stages, from the publisher's editor, Mary Scott, and subsequently from Philip Cooper.

Felix Barker
Watermill House,
Benenden, Kent
1995

The Edwardian era lying as it does within the memory of many of our grandparents has attracted a great number of modern historians, biographers and writers of personal memoirs. There are too many to mention all I have consulted, but I am especially grateful for *Edwardian England 1901-15: Society and Politics* (History Book Club, London, 1972) by Donald Read, the most consistently well-informed and stimulating. Others include:
Edwardian England (Benn, London, 1933), edited by F.J.C. Hearnshaw
Edwardian Promenade (Hulton, Leckhampton, 1956) by James Laver
1914 (Cassell, London, 1959) by James Cameron
1900 End of and Era (Allen and Unwin, London, 1968) by John Montgomery
Victorian and Edwardian London (Batsford, London, 1969) by John Betjeman
The Edwardians (Heinemann, London, 1970) by J.B. Priestley
Edwardian Album (Weidenfeld and Nicholson, London, 1974) by Nicolas Bentley
The Edwardian Era (Phaidon, London, 1987), edited by Jane Beckett and Deborah Cherry

Books on Edward VII often rely too much on constantly repeated legend, and of these perhaps *The King in Love, Edward VII's Mistresses* (Murray, London, 1985) by Theo Aronson is the most eyebrow-raising. More trustworthy are *Edward VII and his Circle* (Hamish Hamilton, London, 1956) by Virginia Cowles, *Edward and the Edwardians* (Sidgwick & Jackson, London, 1967) by Philippe Jullian, *The Life and Times of Edward VII* (Weidenfeld and Nicholson, London, 1972) by Keith Middlemas, and *Edward VII, Image of an Era* (HMSO, London, 1992) by Dana Bentley-Cranch.

For different aspects of Edwardian life these have proved valuable:
Social: *Edwardians in Love* (Hutchinson, London, 1972) by Anita Leslie, *Gilded Butterflies* (Hamish Hamilton, London, 1978) by Philippa Pullar, *The Social Calender* (Blandford, Dorset, 1978) by Anna Spoule and *The Duchess of Devonshire's Ball* (Sidgwick & Jackson, London, 1984) by Sophia Murphy.
Architecture: *A History of Regent Street* (Macdonald and Jane's, London, 1975) by Hermione Hobhouse and *London 1900* (Granada Publishing, 1979) by Alastair Service.
Political and Historical: *Votes for Women* (Faber, London, 1957) by Roger Fulford and *They Saw it Happen* (Blackwell, Oxford, 1960), compiled by Asa Briggs.
Photography: *Crown and Camera: The Royal Family and Photography 1842-1910* (Penguin, Harmondsworth, 1987) by Frances Dimond and Roger Taylor.
British Empire: *The Colonial Office List* (Harrison and Sons, London, 1900 and annually) by W.H. Mercer and A.E. Collins, and *The Colonial Office from Within 1909-1945* (Faber, London, 1947) by Sir Cosmo Parkinson.
Entertainment: *The Theatres of London* (New English Library, London, 1975) by Raymond Mander and Joe Mitchenson.

Miscellaneous Chronology

Aide Memoire to Selected Domestic and Foreign Events

1841   Albert Edward—later King Edward VII—born Buckingham Palace, Tuesday, 9 November.

1849-61   Education of Prince of Wales: after private tutors, briefly at Edinburgh University, Christ Church, Oxford, Trinity College, Cambridge. Studies interspersed with tours of Canada and United States and visits to Ireland, Germany, Italy and France.

1861   Death of Prince of Wales's father, Prince Albert, at Windsor, 14 December.

1863   Prince of Wales marries Princess Alexandra of Denmark at Windsor.

1897   Queen Victoria's Diamond Jubilee celebrated with procession through London. Opening of the Tate Gallery. Opening of Blackwall Tunnel under the Thames.

1899   Start of the Boer War. Natal invaded. Early defeats call for volunteers of which 1000 raised in London before the year's end.

1900   Birth of the Labour Party. Inaugural meeting at Memorial Hall, Farringdon Street, 27 February.

1901   Queen Victoria dies Osborne House, Isle of Wight, 22 January. First London electric tram.

1902   End of Boer War, 31 May. Coronation of Edward VII, Westminster Abbey, 9 August. A.J. Balfour becomes Prime Minister.

1903   Suffragettes formed to demand votes for women. Edward VII visits Paris to establish *Entente Cordiale* with France. Westminster Cathedral opened. First Marks and Spencer store opens at Brixton.

1904   *Entente Cordiale* agreement signed. Covent Garden Flower Market opened. London Symphony Orchestra gives first concert at Queen's Hall, Portland Place. Small film studio opens at Ealing.

1905   Kingsway opened by Edward VII. Chelsea, Crystal Palace and Charlton Athletic football clubs formed.

1906   Landslide victory by Liberals with 130-seat majority over Conservatives at General Election. Victoria station opened as terminus for Brighton and Dover lines. Ritz Hotel opened.

1907   Opening of Old Bailey, Hampstead Tube and Imperial College of Science, South Kensington. Fifth Congress of the Russian Social Democratic Party held in Islington.

1908   Franco-British Exhibition opened at Shepherd's Bush and Olympic Games held at 'White City' stadium. Edward VII visits Russia and extends *Entente* to include Russia in Triple Alliance. Herbert Asquith appointed Prime Minister. Rotherhithe Tunnel, under the Thames, opened. W.G. Grace retires from first class cricket. Freedom of City conferred on Florence Nightingale aged 87.

1909   First Labour Exchanges opened. Lloyd George introduces 'People's Budget' taxing rich, opposed by Tories and rejected by Lords. Port of London Authority set up. New Victoria & Albert Museum opened by Edward VII. First Rugby football match at Twickenham. First Boy Scouts rally at Crystal Palace. Blériot flies Channel and drives in triumph through London.

1910   Edward VII dies at Buckingham Palace, 6 May. Re-designed Mall with Victoria Memorial and Admiralty Arch near completion. Opening of early purpose-built cinemas. Pavlova's first public London performance. First Post-Impressionist Exhibition organized by Roger Fry at the Grafton Galleries. Dr Crippen hanged for murder of his wife.

1911   Coronation of King George V, 25 June. London's first aerodrome opened at Hendon. Siege of Sidney Street. Victoria Memorial unveiled. First appearance of Diaghilev's Russian dancers at Covent Garden.

1912   Sinking of the Titanic. London Museum opened at Kensington Palace. First Royal Command Variety Performance.

1913   First Chelsea Flower Show. Buckingham Palace refaced. Capt Scott and expedition found dead in Antarctic. Suffragette Emily Davison fatally injured at the Derby.

1914   Civil War threatened in Ireland over Home Rule. Archduke Ferdinand assassinated at Sarajevo. Declaration of War against Germany, 4 August. Battle of Mons, 31 August. British and German troops fraternise in No Man's Land on Christmas Day.

Introduction to an Age

By Alistair Cooke

In 1901, a 65-year old Scotsman, born in poverty in a stone cottage, sold his virtual steel monopoly to the United States Steel Corporation for the then prodigious sum of 250 million dollars (today's value would likely be about 15 billion). Andrew Carnegie relinquished his empire with the flourish of a magazine article that ended: 'Farewell, the Age of Iron; all hail, King Steel!'

The piece caught in a phrase the wonders, and fortunes, that had flowed from the new industrial age of the railroads, of oil, of copper, and all-purpose steel; and 'The Age of Steel' was taken up by political and sociological pundits on both sides of the Atlantic. It might have come to define the oncoming decade had not Queen Victoria died in the same year and her long-suffering son and heir come to the throne. The abrupt social transformation of Britain, or, rather, the general sense that there had been one, was so striking that ever afterwards the brief nine years of Edward's reign would be known throughout the English-speaking world as the Edwardian Age.

To appreciate this odd delusion, we have to recall the unique achievement of Queen Victoria, over 60 odd years, in rescuing the British monarchy from popular derision and endowing it with a reputation for private virtue and public respectability.

Shortly after Prince Edward was born, Queen Victoria wrote in her journal: 'I hope and pray he may...resemble his father in every, every respect.' For a while it seemed as if God had listened attentively to the Queen: Edward was an adored and adorable little boy. But before he was out of his teens he began to give off his own vibrations and very soon projected a very un-Albertian image. He loved everything his father had gravely warned him against. By day he shot with a sporty crowd or whizzed to the races in the alarming new horseless carriage. By night, he switched from fast horses to faster women, but (a point seldom made by his detractors) with sufficient discretion to keep from the general public the knowledge that he had an uninterrupted succession of mistresses (whom his adoring and resigned Alexandra called 'my husband's toys'). To the public, he was a welcome change from the sombre and long-reclusive Queen: a genial, cigar-smoking paterfamilias, a teddy bear of a man. The day of his accession practically proclaimed a public holiday from the long grey winter of Victorian restraint.

It did not seem so to everybody. Not to the Nonconformist faithful in the provinces, nor to the upper echelons of government and the court, as Queen Victoria had reformed it. Hearing of Edward's gambling debts, Mr Gladstone feared that 'things could go from bad to worse,' but kept his misgivings to himself. Henry James saw ahead a reign 'made all for vulgarity and frivolity.' To Harold Nicolson, the Edwardians would create 'an age of fevered luxury...They

The Battle of Trafalgar and Nelson's death are remembered on 21 October each year but 1905 was a special occasion. The centenary of the great victory was celebrated by huge crowds. Trafalgar Square was *en fête* and from the top of Nelson's Column hung the 28 flags that spell out the signal: 'England expects every man to do his duty'.

lacked style. They lacked simplicity and their intricacies were excessive and futile.' But such delicate creatures as James and Nicolson led very limited social lives. Neither of them knew, or cared much for, the millions of Londoners outside Whitehall and Chelsea.

Paradoxically, their gloom was rooted in the same error as that of the general middle-class population, which saw a new era of unabashed social splendour, unashamed romance and devil-may-care gaiety. It is the mistake of focussing on the thin and glittering upper crust of a plutocracy as a microcosm of the whole nation. It is as if the whole of America during the same period had been represented by the Robber Barons, whose extravagances and amusements, in much the same way, became the theme of thundering sermons and popular histories, and subsequently the mainstay of motion pictures about the period.

Yet, far from the Marlborough House 'set' and the King's 'toys' and the baccarat scandal, there were 37 million people of every human condition, from the most impoverished to the most cossetted, and an expanding middle class more comfortable than any previous generation of its countrymen: a nation seething with the ferment of new ideas in politics, literature and architecture, and new discoveries in science, industry and medicine, a people whose variety and vitality in the capital city it is the purpose of this book to celebrate.

Fifteen years before Edward came to the throne, two English draughtsmen, W.L. Wyllie and H.W. Brewer, went up in a balloon just west of Westminster Abbey and stayed there long enough to draw, in exact but flourishing detail, a long view of the city, from distant St. Paul's round the bend of the river over four bridges to Westminster and the city to the south. It is a scene of great movement, because of the mantle of cumulus clouds swirling above Turneresque flares of bituminous smoke from every ship and chimney, the soon-to-be-completed docks alive with sliding, puffing freighters. One's first impulse on seeing it today is to shout: 'Quick! Telephone the Environmental Protection Agency!' Wyllie and Brewer were drawing before the word, and the menace, of smog had been heard of, and they certainly did not add the smoke and fumes as artistic touches. They recorded what they saw, and saw with pride. Here was the capital of the Empire, and the smoking freighters were a mere token of the great merchant fleet that brought in the bounteous fruits, the cotton, rubber, sugar, hides, copper, unending raw materials — and shipped out numberless finished goods across the seven seas for the prosperity of the island and the glory of God. It was appropriate that Rudyard Kipling, the troubadour of Empire, should receive the Nobel prize for literature, that Edward Elgar should write a whole series of *Pomp and Circumstance* marches, that John Singer Sargent, the exquisite painter of milady's silks, should be society's portraitist of choice.

But apart from these famous embellishments of the Edwardian legend, there was indeed much going on which, if it did not redound to the glory of God, testified to a decade of astonishing growth and change, of strong protest and daring creativeness in many fields. For the first time, an Education Act gave England a national secondary school system. The Port of London Authority was established. The Liberal party enjoyed its finest (and last effective) hour, introducing a New Deal, 25 years before Franklin Roosevelt, with Lloyd George stumping the provinces condemning the South African war, scarifying the landed gentry and introducing unemployment insurance, old age pensions, minimum hours laws and a budget that taxed unearned income. Meanwhile his radical ally, Winston Churchill, padded around the Home Counties urging the abolition of the House of Lords, 'this second chamber as it is — one-sided, hereditary, unpurged, unrepresentative, irresponsible, absentee.' (Churchill's campaign failed, but the Lords lost forever their one great privilege, the veto power over legislation.)

In science, the Nobel prize was awarded to J.J. Thomson for physics, Ernest Rutherford for chemistry, and Sir Ronald Ross for discovering the malarial parasite in a mosquito. An English

In the Pool of London above Tower Bridge barges unload cargoes from a steamship at a time when this section of the Thames was lined with warehouses.

physicist, Oliver Heaviside, discovered the atmospheric layer that could help conduct radio waves. The establishment of the Metropolitan Water Board finally eased the threat of typhoid fever (which had killed Prince Albert and brought his son Edward to the brink of death).

A literature of protest was very much alive: George Bernard Shaw was at full throttle, with his Life Force and denunciations of any form of government other than Socialism; John Galsworthy recruited his dramatic gifts in the cause of prison reform; H.G. Wells was beginning to see the division of a prosperous society into an upper crust of the idle and a subterranean population of slaves.

The London Symphony Orchestra was founded, and so was Everyman's Library. Cinemas were licensed as legitimate theatres. London, with its four and a half millions, was now the world's biggest city, and host to the Olympic Games.

Most of this creative energy and industrial might would, however, soon be arrested or diverted to more desperate ends, because of a paranoia that gradually but steadily overtook two nations: Britain and Germany. Historians differ, and probably always will, about the time and place the delusion first took hold, when the Great Spy Scare turned, in both countries, from hearsay to fear to a rampaging conviction. Throughout the Edwardian decade there was almost weekly news of European terrorists fleeing the scene of their crimes and stealing into Britain, because, as several newspapers loudly complained, lax espionage laws made the country a safe haven for spies and terrorists. (Joseph Conrad's *Secret Agent* was based on an actual attempt to blow up the Greenwich Observatory.) On the German side, even King Edward's tours of continental spas and pleasure resorts were taken to be scouting expeditions for the encirclement of Germany!

The lack of traffic and unhurried tranquility of this scene on Westminster Bridge makes it seem as if time has stopped. At a quarter past eleven according to Big Ben, this presumably is an ordinary week-day morning in Edwardian London.

There was one person more than another, in Britain, who spread this chauvinist panic: a long-forgotten, demented popular novelist, William Le Queux, who sold a million copies at home and abroad of his 1909 fictional account of the coming German invasion of Britain: *Spies of the Kaiser*. In it he traced a network of 5,000 German spies scattered in tactical locations around the British Isles. This fantasy was elaborated in such persuasive detail as to convince a committee of the Cabinet to create the first British secret service. (After Britain declared war on Germany in August, 1914, a score of suspected spies were arrested, but there was not enough evidence to hold more than one of them for trial!)

If confirmation were needed of Le Queux's hysterical thesis, it came in 1911, when the Germans (of all non-seagoing nations) sent a gunboat to a Moroccan port ostensibly to 'protect commercial interests', actually to embarrass the British and the French and to symbolise the Kaiser's insistence, by that time, that Germany must become a first-rate naval power to prevent a British invasion through France. The upshot of this bizarre incident was an uproar in the House of Commons and the providential decision of the government, over furious opposition from the Welsh miners, to convert the fuelling of the Royal Navy from coal to oil. By then, Admiral Fisher and the new First Lord of the Admiralty, Winston Churchill, were convinced that war was inevitable, and the nervous foreign offices of central Europe were already choosing sides for the approaching conflict. A German general published in England a book (*Germany and the Coming War*) in which he correctly predicted the disposition of the opposing forces, assumed the inevitability of war and, indeed, urged the pressing necessity of it 'for the honour and future of the German nation.' In eastern Europe, not greatly fretted over by a Britain pre-occupied with the prospect of civil war in Ireland, the Austrian Foreign Minister practically guaranteed the eruption of a Balkan war by annexing Bosnia-Herzegovina, then, as now, a provocation to Serbian nationalists and a blight on the prospect they yearned after (and still yearn) of a Greater Serbia.

Throughout the last three years of King Edward's reign, all these mutual fears and suspicions and retaliations planted a minefield of anxiety across Europe. It would require only one lunatic incident to set off the charge of the First World War. The lunatic was Gavrilo Princip, a Serbian agitator. The incident was the appearance in the streets of Sarajevo of the heir to the Austrian throne.

As for the legend of Edwardian gaiety and libertinism, George V, after only a week or two as king, closed the book on it in a simple sentence, spoken to one of his father's cronies 'I am not interested in any other wife than my own'.

CHAPTER ONE

Victorian and
Edwardian Photography

Edwardian London is a description that rolls smoothly off the tongue, but the actual time-span is not easily defined. The reign of King Edward VII, from 1901 to 1910, was so short that for many who lived through the period it seemed hardly to exist; the so-called Edwardian era disappeared as quickly as a mirage. Yet for all their brevity the 'Edwardian' years have acquired a rich flavour and when applied to London conjure up an imperial capital at the height of its prosperity and influence.

The photographs in this book start in 1897, the year of Queen Victoria's Diamond Jubilee, and extend to 1914, four years into George V's reign, almost without our noticing it. Events overlap; plans for buildings do not recognize regnal years. For instance, Kingsway, which was on the drawing-board at the end of Victoria's reign, was opened by King Edward, and development of the thoroughfare went on long into George V's time. Much the same is true of the Mall. Because London wanted to commemorate Queen Victoria in a truly imposing way the idea was born of a splendid ceremonial route starting with a memorial outside Buckingham Palace and stretching to another memorial, Admiralty Arch. Widening and improving this tree-lined avenue took more than a decade. The memorial outside the palace was not unveiled until 1911 and the arch only just ready for George V to pass under it on the way to his coronation. The extent of 'Edwardian' change can be judged from the view of Fleet Street on the cover of this book. At the turn of the century traffic is seen to be exclusively horse-drawn. But by 1901 the motor car would be in the London streets if only at 20 mph; three years later the petrol-driven taxi threatened the hansom cab; and by 1914 the motor omnibus introduced in 1899 would finally see off the horse-drawn bus. Events and periods merged, so that the Boer War straddled two reigns with Victoria hearing the cheering for the Relief of Mafeking in 1900 and, after her death, Edward celebrating the 1902 peace.

Four Generations. This royal family group was taken by a Dublin firm of photographers in anticipation of Queen Victoria's state visit to Ireland in 1900. Behind the Queen is her son, Edward Prince of Wales, her grandson, the future George V, and her five-year-old great-grandson, who became Edward VIII.

The year of Edward's birth, 1841, coincided almost exactly with the invention of photography and it was only slightly earlier that the Frenchman, Louis Daguerre, had invented the photographic process named after him. When daguerreotypes were first seen in this country they fascinated Queen Victoria and Prince Albert who bought several early examples. Bertie (as Edward was always known in the family) must soon have become aware of how compulsive a hobby photography was for his parents and how they were continually collecting pictures to build up the royal archives at Windsor to a total of 50,000 photographs.

Today's royalty have reason to dislike batteries of photographers and long-range lenses, but Victoria, Albert and Bertie, when he became king, turned publicity to their advantage. They thought it a good thing for their subjects to be familiar with how they looked, and a way of managing this came in the 1850s when a French firm invented 'cartes-de-visite'. These neat, small pictures mounted on pasteboard became the rage, and after they had been going for three years the Queen gave permission for portraits of herself to be sold commercially. Overnight her picture, often displayed in a silver frame, took an honoured place on the nation's mantlepieces. It proved a highly successful exercise in royal public relations.

The death of the Prince Consort in 1861 brought Victoria back to a question that had been much on Albert's and her mind: Bertie's future. The Prince of Wales was only just 20, but the heir to the throne ought to be married as soon as possible; the future of the line must be ensured. In the time-honoured way of arranged royal marriages, Princess Alexandra of Denmark was chosen as his bride after photographs arrived in London that confirmed reports of her beauty and charm.

The couple were married in 1863, and, either by coincidence or by encouragement from Victoria, Alexandra developed an interest in her mother-in-law's hobby. She took up photography sufficiently seriously to go for lessons at the studio of the London Stereoscopic and Photographic Company in Regent Street. She carried a camera around with her whenever possible and built up a fine collection of personal photographs.

Queen Victoria's Diamond Jubilee, the culminating public event of the Queen's reign, was widely covered by photographers. Old though she was, the Queen was still interested in anything to do with cameras. As the procession made its way to St Paul's she could be confident that she was in good hands. The main pictures were being taken by the same company that had given Princess Alexandra tuition. Her Jubilee also carried her into the age of moving pictures. When shown a newsreel of the procession she commented: 'Very wonderful. But,' she added critically, 'a little hazy and too rapid.'

King Edward's coronation, which brings us formally to the start of Edwardian London, took place on 9 August 1902, having been postponed for seven weeks because Edward had appendicitis. At midday the Archbishop of Canterbury placed the crown on the King's head, trumpets sounded, bells pealed and to illuminate what threatened to be a gloomy scene, a blaze of electric lights unexpectedly filled Westminster Abbey.

The London crowds cheering outside knew nothing of the Abbey ceremony until they read ornate prose in the following day's newspapers. Cameras along the route recorded public enthusiasm shown on the journey back to Buckingham Palace, but, as it had been for centuries, everything inside the Abbey at a coronation was a sanctified mystery. The day of the well-concealed photographer, the wireless commentator, the newsreel and the television camera was still in the future.

Because we see reproductions of old photographs years after they were taken we are inclined to assume that they were available at the time. In fact, at this stage people who wanted records of big events had to rely on photographs that were sold as postcards or appeared in magazines like the *Illustrated London News* and the *Sphere*. Glossy magazines were able to print them by half-tone and gravure processes. It was not to be for another five years, around 1907, that photographs appeared regularly in newspapers, the difficulties of reproducing them overcome by using minutely dotted screens.

So intent had his mother been on encouraging photographers that by the start of Edward's reign there were about 50 to whom she had granted Royal Warrants. Holders strove hard to retain their 'Special Appointments'. One of them won Edward's affection for the picture they

Edward VII's coronation. Special stands were built and every window and roof-top crowded with cheering people as the great gilded coach passed to and from the Abbey.

took of Princess Alexandra carrying their daughter Louise on her back. Made into a carte-de-visite this was the most popular ever published and had a sale of 300,000. Another photographer was popular with the King because one of his pictures showed him proud as an emperor at the wheel of a 24 h.p. Daimler.

The best chance of success for photographers in a new century was for family or 'multiple' firms to become big business by opening studios in as many places as possible. One such family firm granted a Royal Warrant was Russell and Sons, whose London studios were in Baker Street and Wimbledon. Starting in Chichester, West Sussex, in the middle of the nineteenth century, they were a truly family firm with three sons carrying on the work of James Russell, the founder. Their history is particularly well known to the author because a daughter of Thomas Russell, one of the sons, was my mother. Breaking away from her family she came up to London in her late teens (an unusually independent move for a young woman of that period) and in Victoria Street during the early 1900s as Patricia Russell made a name for herself as a portrait photographer. Leaving the Sussex studios in the care of Thomas and another brother, John, the eldest, photographed Edward as Prince of Wales at Marlborough House and travelled as far as Russia to take pictures of most of Europe's crowned heads.

Styles in photography change, and the unmistakable revolution in the early 1900s was brought about by photo-journalism. As soon as newspapers started to publish photographs a new circulation war broke out in Fleet Street. The press photographer with his left shoulder sloping under a bag of heavy plates, his long raincoat buttoned against street corner winds, may not have looked glamorous but he became the pictorial recorder of the age and seemed to be found everywhere. These pioneer Fleet Street and royal photographers, many of them anonymous, played a large part in bringing Edwardian London to life in the pages to come.

Below As princess, and later queen, Alexandra, a keen photographer, is here using a No. 1 Kodak, the earliest of the easily manageable box cameras with roll films. She took professional tuition, and as Queen published a book of her photographs. Her daughter, Princess Victoria, also made photography a pastime and, like her mother, exhibited her work.

Right Cameras were everywhere along the royal route for Queen Victoria's Diamond Jubilee and one of their most notable pictures was of the Queen at the steps of St Paul's with the Prince of Wales, one of the mounted military figures in the foreground. Victoria was camera-conscious and alert to the best angles from which to be photographed. Raising her parasol and looking up, she is perhaps giving cameramen perched high on Ludgate Hill buildings a chance to see her face.

Opposite A few years into the century, photography had become a popular hobby, with Kodak, a name synonymous with cameras, here advertising the ease of taking pictures and changing film in the window of their shop at 59 Brompton Road, Kensington, around 1905. Signs offer free instruction in photography, a Kodak competition and a folding pocket camera for £4 10s.

In the period when sitters might move during longish exposures, photographs—especially portraits—were improved by retouching, generally carried out with a fine brush on the negative. In 1907 a team of girls is shown working on the delicate task.

By the turn of the century photographers were
familiar figures at great events. One is seen here
outside St Paul's taking pictures of volunteers coming
up Ludgate Hill on their return from the Boer War.

Newspapers began to publish photographs regularly
from 1908. At the Olympic Games at White City that
year a cameraman was so close to the finishing tape
that Dorando Pietri can almost be heard gasping for
breath. The little Italian runner was first across the line
but was disqualified for being helped.

Outside Victoria Station in July 1909 cameras were
ready to greet the Frenchman Louis Blériot who, after
being the first man to fly the Channel, drove
triumphantly through London accompanied by Lord
Northcliffe, whose *Daily Mail* awarded him a prize of
£1,000.

Above In the dock at Bow Street Police Court in 1910 Dr Hawley Harvey Crippen and Ethel le Neve are commited for trial after the murder of Belle Elmore, Crippen's wife, whom he poisoned and buried under the cellar floor of his house, No 39 Hilldrop Crescent, Islington. He was hanged; she aquitted as an accessory after the fact. Photography was permitted in law courts until 1925.

Left At the White Star Lane office in Trafalgar Square there is a stunned reaction as newspaper readers learn of the loss of the *Titanic*, which sank after hitting an iceberg in April 1912. Next day reports suggested there had been a shortage of lifeboats and that priority was given to first class passengers. This was subsequently refuted. More than 1,500 out of 2,200 people aboard died.

CHAPTER TWO

London,

Centre of the Empire

At the bottom of Whitehall a vast new building went up towards the end of the nineteenth century. It was likened not unfairly to a Venetian palace. To create this florid Italian palazzo the south side of Downing Street was demolished and three neighbouring streets sacrificed. Part of this formidable new edifice was occupied by the Foreign Office, by the Colonial Office on the Downing Street-Whitehall corner, and by the India Office, overlooking St James's Park, which was even more impressive and spectacular in design.

Had the architect, Sir George Gilbert Scott, and his colleague, Matthew Digby Wyatt, purposely set out to symbolize the British Empire they could hardly have done better. The Prime Minister, Lord Palmerston, had insisted on a Renaissance classical style to which Scott conformed. Entrusted with the interior of the India Office, Wyatt stopped short at going to the Taj Mahal for his model but contrived a magnificent Durbar Court with a marble floor simulating the pool of an Indian water garden. Crescent stars of India and portrait busts of famous Anglo-Indian Empire builders decorated the walls. From East India House in the City of London marble statues of Charles Cornwallis, Eyre Coote and other imperial heroes were brought to Whitehall to decorate the 'Gurkha Stairs'.

After the small overcrowded Colonial Office across the road at No. 12 Downing Street, the new premises were palatial. At the time of the move there was a staff of only half-a-dozen hard-pressed clerks and a total establishment of 125 to administer an Empire that occupied one fifth of the earth's surface and held sway over 416 million people. This staff had soon to be increased but in those early days sixteen clerks (termed Second Class) worked four to a room. They wrote careful minutes in a copperplate hand and the scratch of pens was only broken when the first 'Lady typewriter', as she was called, began tapping on her machine in 1887. By the end of the century the typing staff had increased to 24 under the Supervisor of Copying into whose holy of holies no man was allowed to enter. Shorthand dictation was kept to a minimum in the new Colonial Office where the atmosphere after the move had only slightly changed from that of a gentleman's club or university Senior Common Room.

In the new environment much was done to preserve old methods. Coal fires in small grates were still regarded better than radiators. Historic relics were carefully moved into the office of the Secretary of State. One was an eighteenth-century chimney-piece (said to have witnessed the chance and only meeting of Nelson and Wellington); another was a large globe, yellowed by varnish, outdated but revolving on its axis to reveal the extent of the Empire. This was supplemented by a large walnut bureau attached to the wall with long drawers from which rolled up maps could be lowered. Inscribed in gold lettering on the bureau were the names of countries under British possession which today have a proud, if outdated, ring.

The Grand Staircase of the Foreign Office given a tropical look for a gala occasion in the late 1890s.

In 1901 Britain's responsibilities extended over more than 40 colonies. Protectorate powers were exercised over territories as remote as Sarawak and places such as Negri Sembilan in Malaya that took a little finding on the roller map. Seventeen of the forty odd names had been part of the Empire since Napoleonic times and by the beginning of the twentieth century British territories encompassed 11,500,000 square miles. Royal Navy warships were anchored around the world; 'gunboat diplomacy' was no empty phrase. The Mediterranean was patrolled from Gibraltar, the Indian Ocean from Cape Town and Mauritius. Since 1818 Britain had commanded the entrance to the South China Sea from Singapore. Demerara, thought of by most people as brown sugar, was in fact part of Georgetown that assured British authority in the Caribbean.

The Empire was so large that desk-bound officials in Whitehall frankly admitted to a serious lack of local knowledge. 'Where on earth is *that*?' we can imagine a puzzled voice asking when faced with a question about We-hai-wei. Would even the roller maps show one of the last among the country's Victorian acquisitions? Files had to be consulted to reveal that We-hai-wei (size 285 square miles, pop. 123,700) was on the Shantung Peninsular of mainland China. Astutely leased from the Chinese in 1898 Britain was using it as a coaling station and also a naval base from which the China Sea could be observed.

Decisions were intolerably delayed, and the Colonial Office always blamed the Treasury, which was proverbially accused of holding up payments for the least expenditure. While procrastination affected efficiency there was also a feeling among Liberal politicians that Britain had as much Empire as the nation could conscientiously embrace. A Colonial Office policy of 'letting matters drift until we have to interfere' sometimes resulted in unanswered cables. This negligence appears to have decided the vexed question of New Guinea. Australia wanted

'A kind of National Palace' was Sir George Gilbert Scott's description of the building he and Matthew Digby Wyatt designed for the civil servants who administered the British Empire. Stretching from Whitehall to St James's Park, it housed the Colonial Office, Home Office, Foreign Office and the majestic India Office, the west side of which is here reflected in the park's lake by Duck Island.

Britain to annex part of the country, and when the Governor of Queensland received no answer to cables he acted on his own account. The outcome was to prevent newly-discovered gold mines falling into German hands.

Acquisitions of the Empire came about unobtrusively. If people thought about them at all, there appeared no cause for uneasy consciences; things had come about not by anything so unseemly as greed: the British had simply followed the pioneering and exploring traditions of their ancestors. Yet, in effect, London, a city of four and a half millions, was ruling over four hundred millions and doing so with quiet assurance from behind the innocent grey facade of the Colonial and India Offices.

During seven years as Colonial Secretary, between 1895 and 1903, Joseph Chamberlain advocated closer economic ties with the Empire and suggested that some of the prosperity taken out of it should be given back, but his efforts were less successful than his enthusiastic utterances might indicate. He continually banged the drum and lent his considerable oratorical powers for imperial preference. In his last public speech in 1906 he sounded rather more the jingoist than calm policy maker. 'England without an Empire!' he exclaimed, 'Can you conceive it? England would not be the England we love.'

But other voices were being raised that threatened the euphoric optimism of Edwardian London. A year earlier a strange little pamphlet appeared called *The Decline and Fall of the British Empire*. It was anonymous and darkly rumoured to have emanated from Japan. Britain's enfeebling faults were enumerated and the main cause for downfall (mercifully not expected

The Durbar Court of the India Office decorated for receptions and state occasions at the time of the Coronation in 1902. The carpeted gangway partly hides the marble floor, which was designed like the pool of an Indian water garden.

until the year 2005) was the country's inability to defend itself. This was echoed later in the decade by H.G. Wells who asked rhetorically: 'Will the Empire live? What will hold our Empire and the British together?'

It might have been expected that the answers to such alarming queries would have been found at the Port of London where the arrival of goods from the Empire was a measure of prosperity. Photographs of the period certainly show busy porters in bulging warehouses along the five miles from Tower Bridge east to Barking. However, statistics indicate that as far as imports from our dependencies were concerned things were not as rosy as they might have been.

One welcome addition to the table of the prosperous Edwardian householder was New Zealand mutton. Refrigeration (first on a sailing ship in 1889, and then by steamer) brought cargoes of 'Canterbury Lamb' into the docks to be sold for as little as 7½d per lb. Wool from Australia was also plentiful, and between 1909 and 1913 Australia sent eight per cent of the wool the country needed. India and Ceylon naturally supplied all the nation's tea. A more serious shortcoming was cotton. Less than half the cotton required by Lancashire looms came up the Thames from overseas. Only 15 per cent of coffee arrived from the Empire and until the Gold Coast plantations expanded the Empire provided only half of the cocoa needed. London Docks, nearest to the City, were piled high with tobacco from Borneo, rubber from Malaya and ivory from Ceylon, but these, like ostrich feathers from South Africa, were exotic, comparatively small imports.

Commercially Britain may have been a bit negligent in developing the potentialities of the Empire, but it gave the nation a comfortable feeling to know that all those overseas territories existed, that there was so much red spread across the atlas of the world. An unequalled opportunity to see this power brought to life was provided by Queen Victoria's Diamond Jubilee. Probably never before (or since) have so many Union Jacks been waved, so mighty a clash of military brass reverberated through London's streets, such a display of exotic uniforms assembled from all over the world. Nearly 47,000 British and Colonial troops took part. Contingent after contingent went by to the blare of martial music, their polished breastplates gleaming. At an occasion like this the small squeak of the subversive Japanese pamphlet that was to be published a decade hence would have been drowned in the roar of the crowd.

On the day of the Diamond Jubilee, 22 June 1897, the idea that one day the sun would set on the British Empire was unimaginable, but two years later the Boer War came as the country's first indication that all was not for the best in the best of all possible empires. Until the autumn of 1899 there was an implicit belief that, as a newspaper put it, the Empire had 'one heart, one head, one language, one policy'. This comfortable assumption was suddenly disrupted by news that in far away South Africa 'a stubborn breed of Dutch peasants' were 'revolting against the just sovereignty of the Queen'. Put differently, Boer settlers maintained that the Transvaal was Dutch and wanted to end British control.

With an insular incapacity for taking events abroad seriously, it was not until news came of military reverses towards the end of the year that the country became alarmed; and then only faintly; surely bearded farmers, even with Bibles in their saddlebags, would be no match for gallant boys in khaki. Soon painful news arrived that these farmers were expert marksmen and fine horsemen who, with a knowledge of the fighting country, were outmatching the outnumbered British troops. Defeats in battles and the besieging of Ladysmith, Kimberley and Mafeking meant a call for more men. Before Christmas there was an appeal for 1,000 volunteers. For the first time civilians, as opposed to regular soldiers, were asked to serve abroad. Within a day London Scottish territorials had 100 men ready to leave and there were many

Sacks of cinnamon ready for inspection by City merchants at a warehouse in London Dock in 1903.

more anxious to take the Queen's Shilling. It promised to be a wonderful lark as shown by the Guards' farewell supper menu — 'Compo Soup', 'Mafeking Mutton', and 'Boer Whines'.

London raised its own special corps, the City Imperial Volunteers. The C.I.V.s were drawn from young men working in the area of the Mansion House. They were financed by a fund of £25,000 raised by the Lord Mayor (and matched by Lord Rothschild). A shipowner promised a troopship to carry 550 officers and men. The 'City's Own' with special bands round their 'Buffalo Bill' hats marched off from the Mansion House via the Temple on their way to the embarkation train at Nine Elms. Each received the freedom of the City. Keenness was shown by those with bicycles who came along with their own machines. Not at first as a soldier, Winston Churchill, then 26, went out to South Africa to be a correspondent for the *Morning Post*. Slightly wounded and taken prisoner, he escaped and was commissioned in the Imperial Light Horse before returning to England and entering politics in 1900.

The Boers' skilful guerilla tactics meant that the war was to stretch on until 1902 and into Edward VII's reign. But before that, there were such victorious highlights as the Relief of Mafeking in 1900 when London went mad. Crowds thronged Trafalgar Square and 20,000 converged on the Mansion House, cheering, shouting and blowing whistles. Union Jacks were waved and 'B-P' buttons were worn in honour of Baden-Powell, the defender of Mafeking. 'Good-bye Dolly Gray' competed with 'Rule Britannia' as the most chanted song, but jingoism was sometimes muted. After Ladysmith Arnold Bennett confided in his *Journal*: 'Such praise of ourselves as a nation, such gorgeous self-satisfaction and boastfulness are to me painful.' Painful, too, were the casualties during the 31 months of the war. Of the 448,725 men of all ranks who fought on the British side 5,774 were killed in action, a further 2,018 died as a result of wounds and 13,350 died from disease. Boer losses (out of a total believed to have been about 60,000) were fewer than 4,000 killed.

Mounted Rifle contingents from Australia and New Zealand are among the colonial troops taking part in the Diamond Jubilee procession. They are passing crowds in Pall Mall East at the bottom of Haymarket.

A statue of General Gordon, killed while attempting to maintain British rule in the Sudan, was raised at the bottom of Charing Cross Road in 1902. It stood here briefly until taken to Khartoum, the scene of his killing on the palace steps. The statue was brought back to England in 1959.

London remembers the Boer War with several statues. On Horse Guards Parade is a memorial to Field Marshal Lord Wolseley; another is to Lord Roberts who replaced Wolseley as Commander in Chief; and one was raised to his successor Lord Kitchener. South Kensington rather than Whitehall has been chosen for Lord Baden-Powell whose statue is fittingly near the Boy Scouts' headquarters. A fifth statue is altogether more unexpected. Mahatma Gandhi served on the British side during the war and, although not specifically for that, has a memorial in Tavistock Square, Bloomsbury. Gandhi formed an ambulance unit of Indians in South Africa and, for leading it, he was mentioned in despatches and awarded a medal. The logic behind his seemingly surprising pro-British action was that if Indians were to claim the status of British subjects they must undertake the same obligations.

The Colonial Secretary's room. Along the far wall
were kept the rolled-up maps of the Empire, which in
the Edwardian era included Canada, Newfoundland,
Mauritius, Papua, Hong Kong, the Malay Peninsula,
North Borneo, India, Jamaica, Australia, New
Zealand and large parts of Africa.

Right For seven years between 1895 and 1903 Joseph Chamberlain held sway as Colonial Secretary. With a monocle and constantly worn buttonhole, he gave the impression of urbanity, but throughout his career he vociferously called for Imperial preference from his Whitehall office.

Left The masculine sanctity of the Colonial office was invaded by the arrival of the first woman typist in the 1880s. The female staff was increased during the Edwardian era to 24 with their appearance and conditions of work probably not greatly different from those seen here at the Royal Society of Medicine, Wimpole Street, in 1912.

Unloading a cargo at London docks. A bale of coir is
being lowered at Millwall Dock. Coir, a coconut fibre,
was used in large quantities in London factories for the
manufacture of rope, cord and matting.

Above Ivory imported from Africa at the Royal
Victoria Dock in 1913.

Right South African ostrich feathers laid out for sale
by auction at Cutler Street Warehouses in the City.
They were brought in through St Katharine's Dock
and 400 tons of them, at a value of £3 million, were
sold each year for Edwardian women's headdresses
and fans.

Bagmen sewing up sacks of sugar at the West India
Docks after their arrival from Trinidad.

The zebra harnessed to a cart in the Blackfriars Bridge
Road may have been one used by a brand tea
company to draw attention to its goods. It was also
around this period that some breeders were crossing
zebras with ponies to improve the strain.

It looks like a stunt, but at London Zoo in 1911 some animals were expected to work for their keep. The camel, a domesticated animal, not difficult to train, pulls the mowing machine without apparent rancour.

CHAPTER THREE

Edward VII Makes Changes

The Boer War was still dragging on, and was to continue for another year when in January 1901 the nation received the news of Queen Victoria's death. The shock was immense. She was 81 but had seemed immortal. It was 64 years since a British sovereign had died and questions of protocol had to be worked out. The Earl Marshal and Lord Chamberlain had some problems about their respective duties but worries were reduced because a few years earlier Victoria had given exact instructions about her funeral. The service, the music, the readings were all specified. The pall on her coffin was not to be black but white as a symbol of her happy reunion with Albert. She was, of course, to lie beside him in the chapel at Frogmore in the grounds of Windsor Castle.

There was no lying in state. London felt a little deprived, and since she had died at Osborne House and was to be taken to Windsor all that people would see of her journey from the Isle of Wight was between Victoria and Paddington on a February day in 1901. There was one small personal touch. While the train belonged to the London and Brighton Company, the actual coach carrying the coffin belonged to the Great Western Railway. This was requested by King Edward because his mother had always liked travelling on the Great Western.

As soon as was seemly Edward VII prepared to move from Marlborough House, his home-in-waiting for so long. Buckingham Palace had become neglected; after Albert's death Victoria had not the heart to clear up their belongings. When the shutters were drawn back and he came to look round, the King gave a peremptory order: 'Get this tomb cleaned up.'

Glitter was restored to blackened gilding and tarnished mirrors. Regency furniture, some of it originally rescued from the Brighton Pavilion and Carlton House, was brought out from under dust sheets. The great staircases were recarpeted and large mirrors put at the ends of state rooms and galleries to give the illusion of added length. Chandeliers, sooty from gas, were lowered and wired for electricity.

Rejuvenation came to a long-moribund court. Just as gloom was banished with electric light so levity dusted off solemnity. As soon as court mourning was over the social calendar was resumed and a good deal of stuffy formality swept away. At the first court of Edward's reign in March 1902 about 70 debutantes were presented in record time. As they came to the red-covered dais of the throne room all the ladies simply curtsied and then moved away to the sprightly tunes of Gilbert and Sullivan to which the King was addicted. By this streamlined method not only were the 70 debs quickly despatched but so, in rapid succession on a single evening, were 8 dukes, 9 duchesses, 11 marquesses and their marchionesses, 37 earls, 11 viscounts and 38 lords. Afternoon 'drawing rooms' were replaced by evening events at which

Royal dignity personified by King Edward and Queen Alexandra in full formal dress for a state occasion in 1903.

buffet suppers were served at tables set out with gold plate and with Champagne plentiful. At the first state ball given by Edward VII and Queen Alexandra there were 2,000 guests.

The anxieties about Edward himself took some time to fade. At Victoria's death Henry James wrote: 'We all feel motherless today. We have no more of mysterious Victoria, but instead fat, vulgar, dreadful Edward.' But this harsh judgement was countered by Winston Churchill's more amiable exclamation: 'Gaddzooks, I am glad he has got his innings!'

The public now began to take a closer look at the man whose rumoured escapades might be all right in a Prince of Wales but would hardly suit a king. His public appearances invariably attracted admiration. In his sixtieth year he was putting on weight but the Inverness cape helped to soften the outlines and he managed to give just the right touch of the dandy he had been in his youth — the top hat, worn at a slightly jaunty angle at the races, the feathered Tyrolean cap, the grey felt Homburg (taking its name from the German watering place where he first acquired it).

The 'Edwardian age' has been daubed in unduly gaudy colours largely because the King has been depicted as a gourmet, gambler and womaniser. Edward's reputation as a gourmet is derived from the undeniable fact that he enjoyed food in large quantities three times a day. To this end he had a French chef and as an example of his menus can be cited a favourite course that consisted of turkey stuffed with chicken inside which was a pheasant that contained a woodcock, all this served cold in a pie. Being a gambler meant that he enjoyed going to the races, backed horses and after years of playing baccaret switched to bridge. He liked to win at the rubber and it was his custom to play nightly after dinner but he always paid up with good grace.

With his notoriety as a 'womaniser' we face greater problems because speculation far exceeds facts. Queen Victoria is reported to have worried about her son's moral transgressions, but only to the extent that if rumours of them 'got out' they might corrupt the middle classes. (The upper classes she presumably considered were beyond redemption and the lower classes below recognition.)

Indisputedly Edward had three major liaisons, which went rather further than the inference of his private secretary, Sir Frederick Ponsonby, when he said that the King was never happier than in the company of pretty women. His reputation was not improved by photographs taken abroad in which his woman companion had obviously been painted out before publication. Much scurrilous capital was made from a cartoon in a German magazine showing him (so the caption went) 'comforting wives and widows of men away at the Boer War'.

Edward's first serious infatuation 14 years after his marriage and while he was still Prince of Wales was with Lillie Langtry in 1877, an actress and famous 'postcard beauty' of the period. She came from Jersey, was known as the 'Jersey Lily' and reports of her much discussed beauty aroused Edward's curiosity. The affair appears to have spread over about three years.

Next of the Prince's close favourites was the elegantly aristocratic Daisy Brooke, future Countess of Warwick, who fitted naturally and without scandalous comment into the 'Marlborough House set'. Their weekend meetings were at Daisy's Essex house, Easton Lodge, where Edward arrived accompanied by a retinue of at least nine servants. Even tactful care by a gentlemen-in-waiting, two equerries, two grooms, two gun loaders and two valets cannot have made intimacy particularly easy. Their deep friendship, spread over nine years, ended amicably. The Prince declared his continued affection and Princess Alexandra sent Daisy a small crucifix with a note saying: 'From one who has suffered much and forgiven all.' Rarely can a three-way entanglement have ended in a more civilised manner.

Edward's third and longest-lasting love, Alice Keppel, came into his life in 1898, when he

As Prince of Wales, Bertie cut a dash as a leader of fashion and society. As well as trousers with creases down the sides, he introduced the Homburg hat which he is wearing here and was named after the German spa where he took the waters.

Below Lillie Langtry

Opposite The Countess of Warwick, who was 'Daisy' Lady Brooke when she became attached to Edward, then Prince of Wales.

was still Prince of Wales and lasted throughout his reign. The relationship was conducted with decorum and infinite tact on her side. In arrangements that involved dinners and house parties and annual Easter visits to Biarritz, Mrs Keppel's discretion and charm seemingly prevented Palace resentment and she even established an amenable understanding with Queen Alexandra. Nearly 30 years younger than Edward, she somehow managed to arrange her life to include a handsome and compliant husband as well as children.

Although Edward VII's reign lasted only nine years he implanted so dazzling an image on court life, on the Season and society that the Edwardian decade has come to be thought of as the most extravagant period London has known. Reckless luxury had existed (if in a rather more subdued way) during the old queen's last years, and the spectacular event that symbolically marks the transition between the reigns was the Duchess of Devonshire's Ball in 1897. Old Devonshire House has been demolished but the legend lives on. Queen Victoria was too frail to attend in her Diamond Jubilee year but 700 other guests came to the house in Piccadilly on that July night.

There had been great fancy dress balls in the past, but dressing up had never before reached such magnificence. Guests came as allegorical figures or historical characters who had existed before 1815. This would seem to give considerable range but there was still mortification because there were three Cleopatras, two Queens of Sheba and two Napoleons. No one was left out of the opulent array of costume; even the staff serving supper off Chatsworth gold plate in the garden marquee were dressed as Egyptian slaves.

Alice Keppel with her husband George and their daughter Violet at a garden party about 1908, ten years after the start of Mrs Keppel's relationship with the king.

It is only natural to ask if there was not a darker side to the Edwardian age and, of course, there was. But before the turn of the century the discontent of the poor does not seem to have been so resentful as it was to become. When at dawn after the ball a sumptuously arrayed Duchess of Marlborough decided to make her way home by foot across Green Park, she found herself passing vagrants whom she slurringly described as 'the dregs of humanity'. 'I thought they would hate me,' she recalled 'but some even made compliments to enliven my progress.'

Such dark impending shadows as were cast by economic conditions did not upset the Social Calendar — that 'fine, decorous, expensive Protestant Carnival' as it was derided by the American writer Henry James. The upper classes had a receptive ear to Oscar Wilde's definition that society is 'merely a bore but to be out of it a tragedy'.

Starting with the Private View at the Royal Academy during the first week in May the London Season saw an unflagging procession of social events. On weekday nights when dinner parties and balls did not demand attendance, diversions were provided by Covent Garden, the Royal Military Tournament and the display of flowers in the Temple Gardens staged by the Royal Horticultural Society, all events likely to be attended by King Edward and Queen Alexandra. For a select few, June meant celebration of the Fourth at Eton; there was polo at Hurlingham and the odd day's refuge from town at Epsom, Ascot and Henley.

Before July faded and the Season was formally over there were two occasions at Lord's Cricket Ground, the Oxford versus Cambridge and Eton versus Harrow matches, when it was a sign of distinction to have a picnic luncheon on the roof of the family coach on the boundary. At the tea interval the grass in front of the pavilion was made entrancing and almost invisible by flowing white dresses and twirling parasols. Mlle Sans-Sêne (probably a *nom de plume* and unquestionably a foreigner) dared to comment in her magazine 'how much more tolerable these functions would be without the cricket'.

The three months of the Season were a period of nervous anticipation for debutantes who were to be presented at court. The dress worn by a girl for her presentation was made to precise specifications by a court dressmaker even though in the new reign the creation would be glimpsed only fleetingly by the King and Queen as a result of Edward VII's determination to curtail formalities.

While appearing at the Palace was the most important event in a debutante's 'Coming Out' season, her parents allowed her little respite. On any one night there were more engagements than she could fulfil. Sometimes there were as many as four dances to which a girl was asked on a single night. Deciding which invitation to accept called for great care because she wanted to choose the dance attended by the most eligible men.

For those comfortably settled on the London social scene a great pleasure was the daily parade in Hyde Park. This took place between midday and two o'clock on the Knightsbridge side of the park with carriages converging on the south-east corner of Rotten Row. Here was the opportunity to see and be seen. Those not in carriages enjoyed nodding to passing friends as they paraded up and down or sat chatting under the trees. Others in barouche or landau were restricted to a regulation number of times they could go by. Immaculate coachmen matched their gleaming vehicles and footmen in powdered wigs lent further prestige.

In the new century a shadow spread over the picture of leisured luxury. In the 'People's Budget' of 1909 taxes were put on higher earned incomes and on all unearned incomes. Land was taxed. The threat of death duties developed into a nightmare that the rich had never previously known. As they saw family capital diminish the nobility looked for a new injection of wealth. Some found it across the Atlantic in American brides who became referred to as 'dollar princesses' following the musical *The Dollar Princess* at Daly's Theatre.

The seven-week postponement of Edward VII's Coronation created various problems. A number of foreign royal visitors had to return home. A Great Coronation Banquet for 250 guests was postponed and the caviare and quails put on ice. One function that went ahead in July as planned was a Coronation dinner paid for by the king for poorer Londoners. A few of the 500,000 people invited, and seen here at a severely labelled table, are in Bishop's Park at the north end of Putney Bridge.

Among the earliest of these valuable American imports was Jennie Jerome, daughter of a wealthy New Yorker. Lord Randolph Churchill married her in 1874 and she is best known as Winston Churchill's mother. The 8th Duke of Marlborough also brought home a transatlantic heiress who by all accounts was no great beauty but with an income of some £40,000 a year was able to feed her spaniels on fricassee of chicken with still enough change left over to re-roof Blenheim. There appears to have been no lack of rich American girls ready to cross the Atlantic, and among many other heiresses woven into the Anglo-American tapestry were Cornelia Martin (Countess of Craven), Leonora van Marter (Countess of Tankerville) and Florence Davis (Marchioness of Dufferin and Ava) — all originally from New York.

As well as dollar heiresses, instant aristocrats were being created and old families shook sorrowful heads at the changes to be seen in *Debrett's Peerage*. This volume had swollen from 400 to 2,000 pages by the start of the century, and in one year, 1900, 5 new peerages were made, a life peer was granted a hereditary title; 9 new baronets and 13 privy councillors came into being; 96 commoners were knighted and 155 people made companions of various orders. Although he was against the privileged rich, Lloyd George as Chancellor of the Exchequer showed no qualms about selling honours (in 1909 around £6,000 for a knighthood and £150,000 for a peerage) to swell the fund of the Liberal Party. Uneasily, Edwardian London noted that old standards of behaviour were changing.

Edward VII acknowledges the crowds on his arrival in
London from Windsor on 23 June 1902. The next day
he was operated on for appendicitis—then a serious
operation—and the Coronation ceremony was
postponed for seven weeks.

Right At Westminster Abbey special stands were
erected for the Coronation so that crowds could greet
the arrival of the State Coach.

Above St Martin-in-the-Fields was just one of the buildings *en fête* for the Coronation.

Opposite The triumphal arch put up in Whitehall for Edward VII's Coronation shows its royal inspiration with portraits of the King and Queen. It also served as a tribute to the victorious Boer War Commander-in-Chief, Lord Kitchener, who was just back from South Africa. Canada, which raised the arch, took the opportunity to advertise. On the other side, brightly lit at night, was the slogan; 'Canada Britain's Granary'. Through the arch is a glimpse of the Edwardian War Office (now Ministry of Defence) under construction.

Indian officers were guests on the terrace of the House
of Commons. Troops arrived from all over the Empire
for the Coronation.

A slim, dignified figure, Queen Alexandra wore a
dress of golden tissue, a velvet and ermine robe and
the Imperial crown at the Coronation. The pages
carrying her train were the 6th Earl of Portarlington,
the 6th Duke of Leinster, Lord Vernon, the 6th
Marquess Conyngham, the 5th Earl of Caledon and
the 6th Baron Somers.

At a Buckingham Palace Garden Party a stickler for
sartorial rules noted almost with a sigh of relief in
1911: 'The frock coat is holding its position.' His
thankfulness was short-lived. Within a year or so, as
this photograph (*left*) shows, the tailed morning coat
had largely superseded its square-cut rival. And by this
date carriages, which would have brought many to the
garden party early in the reign, had been replaced by
cars whose chauffeurs wait in the Royal mews (*above*).

All the ornate splendour associated with Edwardian taste blooms in the White Drawing Room of Buckingham Palace as it looked after Edward VII and Queen Alexandra moved in. Queen Victoria's heavy furnishing was replaced by lighter, brighter decoration in the French Empire style. On State occasions this sumptuous white and gilt room in the private part of the palace was used for receptions. Under the glittering, newly electrified chandeliers, guests on their way to the Ballroom were received by the king and queen, who made an appropriately magical entrance by way of a massive mirror (to the left of the fireplace), which swung open to serve a doorway. The portrait over the mantelshelf is of Queen Alexandra in her Coronation robes.

In the refurbished palace the King had a private suite of his own. In the anteroom, leading to a bedroom and dressing room, furniture and oddments were arranged in homely confusion. On the left of the door he kept rows of hats as if for a last-minute decision; formal top hats were to the right, and near the window a large choice of walking sticks. On a square rack were numerous mounted photographs, perhaps cartes-de-visite presented by callers. Conspicuous on an easel was a portrait of his favourite sister, Princess Alice, great-grandmother of the present Duke of Edinburgh.

A debutante would want to keep a record of her dress
and how she looked for her presentation at the Palace.
This studio photograph shows a young Edwardian
beauty in her gown with a long train, all specially
made by a court dressmaker for the occasion.

Spreading ever larger, women's picture hats
dominated the Edwardian fashion scene. They can
rarely have been more spectacular than those worn by
the bridesmaids at the 1907 wedding in St James's
Palace of Eugenie Fanny Eveline Dudley Ward and
Captain Bryan Godfrey Faussett, a royal equerry.
Among the array of presents seen at the Lowndes
Square reception was a silver bowl presented by King
Edward, a diamond scarfpin from the Queen and a set
of waistcoat buttons from Princess Victoria of
Schleswig-Holstein.

Not quite cricket; more a dress parade. Chatting during the tea interval at Lord's, women, decorative under parasols, appear to have taken possession of the ground in front of the pavilion. The match in 1908 could be Oxford vs Cambridge but top hats on some young boys rather suggest Eton against Harrow.

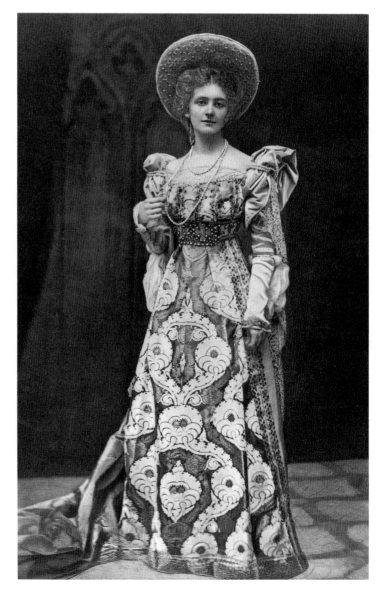

Below In comparison with the countess of Westmorland, the Hon. Mrs George Curzon, American-born wife of the future Lord Curzon of Kedleston, chose a modest costume as Valentina Visconti of Milan.

Above At the Duchess of Devonshire's famous ball in 1897 costumes were of unprecedented extravagance. With a stuffed eagle on her shoulder, the Countess of Westmorland, as Hebe, was admired but found that her dancing was greatly hindered. Margot Asquith came as a snake charmer with a serpent round her bosom, an American guest had electric lights woven into her hair and Edward, then Prince of Wales, paraded a huge Maltese Cross on his sturdy figure.

Extravagant balls continued into Edwardian times and
the most spectacular of all was the Arabian Nights Ball
given annually at Covent Garden. This event
described as 'the most popular of the winter season'
was organized by the Foreign Press Association. In
1913 there were exotic tableaux and parades of
fashionable beauties who appeared in the guise of
jewels. It was an occasion not to be missed by Lord
and Lady Alington, ardent partygoers and partygivers
who had been friends of Edward VII. Among the
revellers, Lord Alington came as Bluebeard.

The greatest spectacle seen in Edwardian London was
the Franco-British Exhibition at Shepherd's Bush,
which opened in May 1908 (*above*; *opposite, below*). It
was the largest show ever held in Britain up to that
time and 8,000,000 visitors came to wonder at the
'White City' as it soon became called. Forty acres of
gleaming wedding-cake buildings were set among half
a mile of waterways. Pre-eminent was the Court of
Honour and an Indian-style palace, with fountains
and bridges round an artificial lagoon.

The White City was visited by President Fallières of France, seen here (*above*) going round the exhibition with King Edward. The occasion put a seal on the *Entente Cordiale* agreement of alliance between England and France that the king had signed with a previous French president four years before.

Photographers delighting in the contrast between slim
dresses and rotund balloons contrived to get
fashionable women in the foreground at the start of
balloon races at Hurlingham in and after 1906.

Opposite Among the many American heiresses who married into the British aristocracy was Consuelo Vanderbilt, wife of the 9th Duke of Marlborough. In her late thirties in 1909, this 'dollar princess' retained legendary beauty. Very tall and slender with swan-like neck and wasp waist she had (so a photographer noted) a tip-tilted nose and pursed smile in a 'minute face as symmetrical as a primrose'. She moved with ceremonial grace and, recalling her wardrobe, he said 'she seemed to spend her life simplifying her silhouette'.

Right The Duchess's renowned beauty was brought to the role of canvasser in politically active Battersea, anyway to the extent of chatting to a local butcher.

Fashionable society strolled and gossiped in Hyde Park during the Season. The rich, and sometimes members of the royal family, bowled in by landaus with footmen in powdered wigs and gleaming equipage.

Appearing in Rotten Row demanded perfect mounts
and impeccable riding habits. There were raised
eyebrows when match-making *nouveau riche* mothers
showed off their daughters in slow-moving open
carriages hoping to attract attention.

CHAPTER FOUR

The Growth of Edwardian London

Comfortable prosperity and the prospect of even more affluence encouraged London's Edwardian development. Great new buildings went up; famous streets changed their appearance; few areas were unaffected except, strangely enough, the City of London and the West End. A Royal Commission report in 1905 outlining City developments during the previous 70 years seemed to declare 'So far and no further'. As for the West End, great landlords were sitting pretty, and only Regent Street was partly altered because of lease changes.

By far the most dramatic development of the reign was Kingsway. Suddenly a great new thoroughfare thrust its way north from the Strand. Here was the answer to hold-ups caused by slow-moving horse-drawn traffic (which could cause congestion just as badly as modern motor vehicles). A major artery to Holborn lined with large rentable buildings appealed to investors, and the London County Council was eager to demolish much of the wretched property that lay in its path. The Council made plans for a straight 100 feet-wide avenue, and eight private architects were invited to submit designs for a monumental crescent at its southern end. There was a general feeling that this new L.C.C. project must have a better design and more sense of purpose than had Shaftesbury Avenue a few years earlier.

A bold concept, Kingsway involved the clearance of 28 acres, mostly slums, but also Wych Street and the south end of Drury Lane, which still had vestiges of overhanging Tudor houses, gabled roofs and galleried courtyards. The creation of the crescent called Aldwych ('Old Town' after a presumed twelfth-century Danish occupation) also required heavy demolition and the loss of four theatres, including the famous old Gaiety; a new Gaiety and the Strand and Aldwych theatres replaced them. The Waldorf Hotel fitted in with the curve of the crescent and had a Palm Court, a growing feature of Edwardian hotels. Bush House, Australia House and India House were originally conceived for the Aldwych crescent but were not to be added until after the Great War.

In Kingsway itself such massive stone-face buildings as Imperial House, Regent House, Windsor House and York House (from one firm of architects, 1911–14) did not dispel the monotony of the long straight street, but a touch of the spectacular and glamorous might have come from the London Opera House halfway up. Conceived by the American impresario, Oscar Hammerstein, the theatre was built in 1911 in French-Renaissance style as a rival to Covent Garden. An ill-starred enterprise, the London Opera House was a failure, becoming a cinema, and then the Stoll Theatre, before being rebuilt in 1960 as the subterranean, spasmodically used Royalty Theatre.

As Victoria Street had shown half a century earlier, a straight street lined with austere build-

At the turn of the century traffic congestion was even worse than at present. Slow horse-drawn vehicles and no pedestrian control led to chaos, as seen here at the converging of six streets by the Mansion House.

The vastly ambitious London Opera House covering nearly an acre of Kingsway between Sardinia and Portugal streets opened in 1911. With a final capacity of 2,420 it was larger by about 300 seats than Covent Garden, which it intended to rival. But it was to survive for only six months as an opera house and lost a massive sum for its sponsor, Oscar Hammerstein. The design sought to capture the right flavour with twelve statues along the front representing Melody, Harmony, Composition, Inspiration, Comedy, Tragedy, Dance and Song.

ings all of roughly the same date and design is not calculated to raise the spirits. The L.C.C. Improvements Committee had a vision of grandeur with their monumental avenue. Sadly they lacked the Haussmann touch. In their defence we have to remember that County Hall engineers were allowed only £5 million for the project, a fraction of the vast sums paid by Napoleon III to Baron Haussmann to improve Paris boulevards.

New century changes to Regent Street came about with alteration to shops. In 1907 many 99-year leases fell in, and shopkeepers decided they must cater for a larger, if less fashionable clientele. With scant regard for Nash's grand design, the Quadrant with its colonnades had long since been demolished. Now the Piccadilly Circus end was rebuilt with a new hotel, the Piccadilly, and an enlargement of Swan and Edgar's, 'The Leading West End Drapers', a 1906 scheme overseen by Norman Shaw, who had retired, but was still the dominant architect of the period. The changes to Regent Street from Waterloo Place to Portland Place that occurred because of lease alterations can be seen in the way Regency-style buildings were replaced by new Edwardian blocks. Charm gave way to the grandiose as seen in Robinson and Cleaver on the corner of Beak Street.

Shops on corners were inevitably crowned by domes. These gave 'importance' to corner sites and were rarely resisted by architects of the day. Domes that were flattened, ribbed, ribboned and pierced with circular windows challenged domes the shape of dish covers. Some were encrusted with so much decoration as to be hardly visible, as on the Y.M.C.A. (1911) on Tottenham Court Road. The dome on the Methodist Central Hall, Westminster, irregular and flighty in the French Beaux Arts manner, seems frivolous on an evangelical building. All may have been belated tributes to Wren but would surely have given him nightmares.

These whimsical fancies showed the unbridled freedom enjoyed by Edwardian architects. When in doubt they reached for their pattern books. Out came swags of fruit, broken pediments, nymphs and cornucopias; pressed into service were mansard roofs ventilated with round skylights, terracotta brickwork and tourelles borrowed from French châteaux.

Nowhere was this exuberance better seen than in the Middlesex Guildhall facing Parliament Square, a building so liberally displaying 'medieval' detail that it has attracted the ironical description of 'Art Nouveau Gothic'. Having to avoid the style of Central Hall nearby, the architects may have thought that they would pay some sort of tribute to Westminster Abbey across the square. Had Hollywood created this pastiche it would have been ridiculed as 'Warnerbethan'; the Abbey can only have regarded it as an unruly puppy.

While in this area we must consider Westminster Cathedral in Victoria Street and the varied reactions it aroused. Whether or not it can claim to be the most outstanding single building to go up in Edwardian London, it is undeniably spectacular. With a 284-feet-high campanile (taller than the towers of Westminster Abbey), a dome 117-feet high and built in material alien to London, red brick banded with white stone, this monument to the Roman Catholic faith was bound to raise controversy. Protestants cynically regarded it as Papist ostentation. Opened in 1903, it was dubbed 'Vaughan's folly' — a reference to Cardinal Vaughan (d. 1903) under whose influence the cathedral was built. Although constructed in a Christian style foreign to London it has gained the affection of English Catholics and has won the reluctant admiration of Londoners generally.

The style most fancied by architects of Edwardian public buildings was High Baroque as represented by the single-domed Central Criminal Court at the Old Bailey (for which George Dance's Georgian Newgate Prison was destroyed) and the two-domed War Office in Whitehall, both of 1906. The grandiose temptations of the time led to extravagances when the Victoria and Albert Museum came to be rebuilt in South Kensington. Heavy expenditure was entailed but would hardly have been thought a fault by Queen Victoria when (at her last public engagement) she laid the foundation stone in 1889; this was, after all, as a prestigious museum of the arts.

'Swan and Edgar's Corner', as the north-western quadrant of Piccadilly Circus was called, and as the elegant shop still looked in 1910. It was rebuilt under Norman Shaw's scheme, which included the new Piccadilly Hotel.

A competition for the new museum was won by Aston Webb, later the President of the Royal Academy, who was then at the start of his highly successful career as an architect. On paper, Webb's five domes, pointed towers and a tiered octagonal cupola looked fine, but when built and viewed from the Cromwell Road, the terracotta front of the building was ostentatious, and yet the total effect strangely mundane. More seriously for a museum, the inside did not work. The richly decorated marble exhibition halls were too large and ornate to show off the delicate treasures they displayed. Within two years of the opening by Edward VII in 1909 it was decided to tone down the interior. 'Disturbing and antiquated decoration' was removed to turn the museum into 'the sublime attic' for beautiful objects it was to become.

The V. & A. may have served as an awful warning; at any rate it appears to have brought about a desirable reaction. Simplicity became preferred to embellishment, and as the century went on this change was to be seen in newly built hotels, shops and gentlemen's clubs. When the Ritz went up in 1906 extravagant decoration gave way to restraint with no more than a slight nod towards Paris and the Beaux Arts movement. The one *coup de théâtre* was the pavement arcade, which brought the Rue de Rivoli into Piccadilly.

Simplicity was all very well but architects felt the need to earn their fees. If Baroque was out, they found a welcome substitute in refined classical design. In 1907 the United Services Club in Pall Mall was built with classical columns peeping out of baroque surroundings and in the following year the Royal Automobile Club, also in Pall Mall, went uncompromisingly Greek with a columned portico and elegant pediment. When it came to building the Edward VII Galleries of the British Museum in 1904 a 'Classical Re-Revival' design (Nikolaus Pevsner's term) won the day over 12 competitors. Facing Montague Place along the back of the museum which escapes the eyes of most observers, John Burnet imposed a line of 20 Ionic columns straighter and more uniform than guardsmen.

When the Ritz was built in Piccadilly in 1905 its most unconventional feature was the pavement arcade—a Parisian touch—which here is partly visible behind a horse bus and motor bus.

Clearly the early Underground railway thought it paid to advertise. By the early 1900s Victoria Station's surface lines were supplemented by the District line stretching out to the east and west. To reach many of the destinations mentioned would have required changing from the underground to existing surface lines.

While this colonnade was being built, Gordon Selfridge from Chicago was starting work on his Oxford Street store. He saw no reason why a store should not vie with a museum. Selfridge also decided on columns, massively larger ones, for his facade. Who Selfridge's principal architect was is not clear; several were involved, with Burnet, the museum designer, among them. Whoever his advisers were, by the time the store opened in 1909 nine columns were in place and finally they triumphantly outnumbered those at the back of the British Museum by two. Rather surprisingly Harrods which might be expected to be very grand indeed has a disappointing main facade (1903) in pink terracotta that falls indecisively between Baroque and Second Empire — but, of course, sports the obligatory dome.

More important than any single Edwardian development was the suburban explosion. London's growing population was pushing outwards, helped by the first electric tram from Hammersmith out to Kew in 1901; then by the Underground with the extension of the District Line to Ealing; and the tunnelling under Hampstead Heath out to Golders Green. Fleets of motorbuses helped the exodus and in the first decade of the century nearly half a million people moved into an ever-extending Greater London.

Breaching the barrier of the Northern Heights and converting a private house into a quaint terminus (Golders Green Station) the emerging Underground turned meadowland into housing estates and in the Finchley-Hendon area alone the number of houses rose by 14,000 during the next seven years. Most houses had the uniformity associated with 'suburban' homes, but some were more rarified. One such scheme was bequeathed with the prestigious (rather than geographically accurate) name of Hampstead Garden Suburb. This was the brainchild of

Dame Henrietta Barnett, wife of a Whitechapel clergyman. Possessed by egalitarian ideals, she decreed there were to be no public houses. Shops were banished to the perimeter and noise was sternly forbidden. Residents should not be concerned with age, class or income. It was all too good to last. When this Edwardian paradise was founded in 1907 Dame Henrietta was starry-eyed but although her garden suburb proved attractive she came to admit that most people were too insular and classbound to live up to her initial hopes.

More truly egalitarian on a working class level was the 1907 Millbank Estate and the Boundary Street Estate, Shoreditch, opened by Edward VII when Prince of Wales in 1900; both were designed by the L.C.C. with the aim of providing a large number of pleasant-looking flats for poorer people.

Hampstead Garden Suburb was an idealised version of all that came to be meant by 'suburbia', a word that found its way into use at the turn of the century. To the chic and comfortable residents of Kensington and Chelsea suburbia was a target for scorn and satire, as a description of Clapham indicates. It was not the architecture but the ethos that came in for sneers. Choosing Clapham as 'the capital of Suburbia', the author of *The Suburbans* (1905), T.W.H. Crossley, saw the place as representing 'the cheapness and out-of-jointness of the times'. To him this was typified by a wide-swinging catalogue of aversions — the gramophone, bamboo furniture, golf, secondary school education, miraculous hair restorers, prize competitions and 'all other sorts of twentieth-century clap-trap'.

In the first 8 years of the century the Council opened 12 major housing estates in Inner London with flats for over 17000 people. The Millbank Estate with its pleasant public garden was completed behind the Tate Gallery in 1907 and built on the site of the demolished Millbank Prison.

Another L.C.C. housing project, the Bourne Estate, was completed in the Clerkenwell Road in 1907. Five storey tenement blocks were built to house 3,900 people. There was a brave attempt to make the building more appealing with seats, lively paving and brickwork and with trees planted on the sunny side of the courtyard.

Writing a year earlier L.T. Hobhouse, clearly an unliberal Liberal, came down heavily on the suburbs on political grounds. He regarded them as nests of middle class complacency and so great an impediment to political progress as to be 'a greater national danger than the slums'. Then in 1909 a third critic of suburbia C.F.G. Masterman conceded (in *The Condition of England*) that fresh air was good for children but he shuddered when he contemplated the mental climate of their parents and gave as examples 'the superficial chatter of the commuter train and of suburban tea parties'. Poor Edwardian Londoner; it is difficult to see how he survived the fatal benefit of the Underground.

Kingsway stretching north from Aldwych to Holborn
involved the demolition of buildings backing onto
Lincoln's Inn Fields on the right, and many small
streets round 17th-century Clare Market on the left.
At this stage of construction the tram tunnel under the
street is still exposed.

Above The opening of Kingsway by Edward VII, who is in the carriage under the awning, on 18 October 1905.

Left The tram tunnel linking the Embankment with Holborn from which passengers could emerge at intervals in Kingsway was a good idea but had snags. Low headroom meant that the trams had to be single-deckers and this required a shuttle service with passengers changing at each end.

Cheering crowds lined Westminster Bridge Road on 5 May 1903, when the first electric tramway in the London County Council area came into existence. In the absence of the King, who was on a visit to Scotland, the Prince of Wales (the future George V) inaugurated the service at the controls of a specially painted white tram festooned in evergreens. The royal party, which included Princess Mary and two young princes, enjoyed the luxury of seats upholstered in blue and pink. Their ½d fares were solemnly collected by an official in a top hat. The five-mile journey was to Tooting and a following procession of 50 more mundane trams carried 2,500 invited guests. The L.C.C. could not claim to be the first in the revolutionary change away from horse-drawn trams. As early as July 1901 an electric tram had travelled from Shepherd's Bush to Acton, and there were already several tentatively operating west London routes. To start with, the electrified trams were restricted to four main roads into London but by 1905 twenty-eight tramways criss-crossed the whole of London providing, it was claimed, 'the most efficient and cheapest means of street conveyance'.

This view of the west side of Aldwych shows the development of the crescent in 1908. The Waldorf Hotel is already up, with the Strand and Aldwych theatres at each end. They overlook a devastated area that included four theatres, Wych Street with its Tudor buildings, the lower end of Drury Lane, fourteen public houses and Holywell Street. Bush House and other large buildings in the Aldwych were not to be finished for another twenty years.

Right Early photographs of guests inside hotels are rare. This one taken in 1898 at the Hotel Cecil in the Strand, Europe's largest hotel (the present Shell-Mex House site), was at a farewell dinner to Lord and Lady Curzon of Kedleston. Lord Curzon, the recently appointed Viceroy of India, is on the centre table facing the camera with the Duchesses of Devonshire and Rutland, the Duke of Portland and Lady Warwick.

Northumberland Avenue between Trafalgar Square
and the Embankment had two large hotels in 1905,
both owned by the same hotelier. The Grand had 500
bedrooms, while the Metropole was popular with
Edward when Prince of Wales. Guests at the
Metropole enjoyed the facility of a horse brake for
trips to Richmond and Kew.

With horse omnibuses, hansom cabs, carriages, carts
and only a scattering of pedestrians, the brick-paved
Quadrant in Regent Street has an almost countrified
look on this March day in 1905.

Dickens and Jones was opened in Regent Street's early years and came to this site on the corner of Oxford Street in 1833. Seen here in 1910 are the ample sunblinds needed to protect goods and the delicate complexions of women shoppers. Styling themselves linen drapers, the store sold all ladies' fashions. The curved corner with columns is believed to have been part of John Nash's original Regent Street design.

Shopping at the Oxford Street corner of Regent Street
in 1908. Like a number of prosperous stores Peter
Robinson spread over several shops. One of them was
their Mourning Warehouse with 'all grades of
Mourning kept in stock for immediate use'.

From being a simple shop Harrods had grown by 1903 into a large, famous store, with a terracotta facade overlooking Brompton Road. The store's great innovation was to install the first moving stairway for customers.

Opposite Pontings in Kensington High Street in 1912 displays artificial fruit and flowers, feather plumes, boas and fur coats on the floor above.

The west end of Selfridges when nine of the columns
facing Oxford Street were ready for the 1909 opening.
The rest of the colonnade, with columns
outnumbering those on the back of the British
Museum, was built later with the extension and
completion of the store further east.

At Barkers in Kensington High Street in 1913 there is
a department with a blinding variety of electric lamps
with Art Nouveau shades, electric fires and even an
electric vacuum cleaner.

In his design for Middlesex Guildhall in Parliament Square between 1906 and 1913, the architect James Gibson embraced medievalism with an astonishing lack of inhibitions. Gothic motifs sprout everywhere. Upper dormer windows are topheavy with detail. The tower defies sane architectural definition. The main doorway combines a history lesson with rampant symbolism: the sculptor, H.C. Fehr, depicts the abbots of Westminster receiving a charter from Henry III or it may be Henry IV. The keystone for the arch embraces the Great Hall at Hampton Court with the figures of Law on either side, while the larger figures in flanking niches are Justice and Prudence. The flamboyant coat of arms of Middlesex County Council provides the crowning glory.

The Royal Automobile Club, Pall Mall, built in 1908
was in the neo-Classical style, which was replacing the
earlier Edwardian tendency towards Baroque.

Among Edwardian buildings one of the most spectacular was Deptford Town Hall in an area not noted for its ambitious architecture. The central oriel window is supported by an over-enthusiastic pair of caryatids, and Deptford's past maritime glory is symbolised by statues of admirals, while the decorative panels include shells, anchors and other seafaring devices.

Flower sellers at the upper end of Regent Street near
Oxford Circus.

This Hammersmith butcher displays no vegetarian
inhibitions at his King Street shop about 1910.

With the creation of Aldwych and demolition of part of the Strand, a new Gaiety Theatre was built on the Strand corner. This was opened in November 1903, only four months after the closure of the old Gaiety. It is seen here in 1913 (during the run of *The Girl on Film* yet one more of the 'Girl' shows staged by George Edwardes). The two early omnibuses, contrasted with the two horses drinking from a trough (1910) in the same part of the Strand, shows the transition from earlier to later Edwardian London.

The imposing front (*above*) to the rebuilt Victoria &
Albert Museum opened in 1909. Aston Webb's
building has five domes, pointed towers and this tiered
octagonal cupola, seen from the Cromwell Road side.
The museum was matched by an over-ornate interior
(*opposite*) that, until modified, did not show off all the
exhibits to their best advantage.

In Hampstead Garden Suburb there was a rule that to
foster neighbourly friendship there should be no high
hedges and that houses should be no more than fifty
feet apart. The family here are separated by only a low
wire fence from the people next door. To attain
proximity without overcrowding there were to be just
eight houses to the acre, mostly in neo-Tudor, William
and Mary or some other style blessed by the Arts and
Crafts Movement. The Tenants' Social Council put
great emphasis on giving children playing space and
small garden plots that they could cultivate themselves.

Seven years before the middle-class Utopia of
Hampstead's garden suburb was conceived, the
London County Council was making big plans to
provide housing for the poor. A notorious slum area
west of Shoreditch High Street was demolished and
laid out in 1900 as the Boundary Street Estate. Roads
between five-storey housing blocks radiate from a
raised, unusually designed recreation space named
Arnold Circus.

Westminster Cathedral, so alien to the London of
1903, for some time attracted ridicule, and the
campanile was likened by Frederick Rolfe (a Roman
Catholic writer rejected for the priesthood) to 'a pea-
soup and streaky-bacon coloured caricature of an
electric light station'. In more measured terms it was
in a richly decorated Byzantine style as the doorway at
the opening ceremony shows (*opposite*).

'Edwardian Baroque' is typified by the dome, the
varied architectural styles and the red granite used by
Robinson and Cleaver in 1910 to give 'importance' to
the Beak Street corner of their shop. This contrasts
with Liberty's neo-classical shop to the right and the
stretch of lower buildings, left, which retain something
of their original Regency style.

Yet another dome, so heavily decorated as to be
almost invisible, was built in 1911 for the corner
premises of the Y.M.C.A. in Tottenham Court Road.

Covent Garden, then privately owned by the Duke of
Bedford, was at the height of its activity as a fruit,
flower and vegetable market in Edwardian times.
Floral Hall with arched glass roofs is on the right, and
another hall, Jubilee Market, was completed in 1904.
Nearly 1,000 Covent Garden porters competed with
each other over the number of baskets they could
carry piled on their heads.

Crisp or Chrisp Street, Poplar (the 'h' appears to be optional) had an outdoor market thronging with East End shoppers in 1904.

CHAPTER FIVE

Edwardians
Enjoy Themselves

Entertainment and the spread of popular culture seemed to have few limits in the year leading up to 1914. Looking back this can be construed as a desperate search for pleasure under the impending shadow of the Great War, but in fact few people had premonitions of the horrors to come; even when hostilities broke out they were treated at first rather as a lark. In Edwardian London people were simply out to have a good time.

In response to the call for entertainment 15 theatres were built between 1900 and 1913. New concert halls opened and at the Queen's Hall, Langham Place, seating was pulled out to double the shilling standing room for Henry Wood's first Promenade Concerts. At the newly-built London Hippodrome the public fancy was tickled by water spectacles, circuses and the Russian ballet. When a revue *Hello Rag-Time!* arrived from America showgirls came out on a 'Joy Plank' that projected over the stalls.

New music halls sprang up all over London with audiences responding to the rough gusto of Marie Lloyd and George Robey. Films made at improvised studios in suburban back gardens flickered onto screens and by 1910 London had 300 cinemas. Art was opening up new frontiers. At the Grafton Galleries the public first faced with the work of Cézanne, Matisse and the Post-Impressionists declared it 'either an extremely bad joke or a swindle'. These varied pleasures still left time for such Edwardian crazes as tea-dances and roller skating.

London, it seemed, could not have enough theatres. Between 1900 and 1907 a new theatre was built each year, except 1902. Of these four were in Shaftesbury Avenue and, added to the Palace and the old Shaftesbury Theatre (where *The Belle of New York* lingered indefinitely), now made the street synonymous with showbusiness. They were the Apollo; the Globe (now the Gielgud); the Queen's; and at the Holborn end, the Princes (now the Shaftesbury).

As if the West End would die without a George Edwardes theatre to attract stage door Johnnies an urgent remedy was needed when the old Gaiety in the Strand was demolished in 1903. A new Gaiety went up on the corner of the Strand and Aldwych within four months. The opening show, *The Orchid*, starring Gertie Millar, made the mistake of not having the word 'girl' in the title but queues formed at 5a.m. and King Edward and Queen Alexandra were in the royal box on the first night.

Determined to beat its own track record, London went on to create four other new theatres in the single year 1911. The most famous was the Victoria Palace opened by Alfred Butt who as an act of homage put a statue of Anna Pavlova on the dome. Two others, previously mentioned, were the London Opera House in Kingsway, which never fulfilled its hopes of glory, and the Princes, which made great play of having a sliding roof to enhance ventilation. The fourth was

A flashlight photograph catches an unusual West End audience at the turn of the century. The occasion was a charity matinee staged by Charterhouse School at the Haymarket Theatre in June 1899. Women in the packed audience are wearing cumbersome hats and high-peaked bonnets, which, because they interfered with people's vision, were normally restricted to the rear part of the Circle.

the Regent, entangled among the lecture halls of the Polytechnic College, Upper Regent Street.

There were actors and producers to match the bricks and mortar. Among them the actor-manager came to typify an Edwardian trend. Two years before the Diamond Jubilee Henry Irving became the first actor-manager to be knighted; Charles Wyndham came next in the new century; Herbert Beerbohm Tree, Johnston Forbes-Robertson and George Alexander followed just a few years apart, each bringing a distinctive flavour to the theatres, plays and parts they chose. Tree at His Majesty's became famous for spectacular Shakespeare. Curiosity drove play-goers to see if it was really true that Tree had live rabbits hopping about a wood near Athens in *A Midsummer Night's Dream*. (The reliable report is that, ignoring the lovers, the rabbits happily nibbled stage grass.)

Mid-Victorian melodrama still had adherents, and audiences held their breaths when the hero fought the villain for possession of a jewel in a balloon over Hampstead Heath in *The Great Ruby* (1898) or a weir burst and a troopship sank in *Sins of Society* (1907). But empty bombast was on the way out. More to the public taste was realism and the kind of natural acting in 'cup-and-saucer comedies' for which Alexander was admired at the St James's.

Giving the theatre of the period an even greater reputation was the New Drama. To the Royal Court, Sloane Square, came a new generation of playgoers to see Harley Granville Barker's productions of Bernard Shaw, a John Galsworthy social drama and tragedies by Euripides. Among Shaw's seven plays at the Court was his comedy *John Bull's Other Island*,

The small and elegant Bechstein Hall, seating 600 for concerts, opened in 1901 and was approached by a passageway leading from Wigmore Street. Facing the street were showrooms for the musical instruments made by Bechstein's, who had their own delivery vans. The concert hall, named after the German, Carl Bechstein (and completed the year after he died), was altered during the Great War to the Wigmore Hall.

which, although it dealt controversially with Irish Home Rule, was held acceptable for the King to see. *Press Cuttings* (1909) was a different matter. Shaw's comedy about the suffragettes, with Asquith and Kitchener as identifiable characters, failed to get past the Lord Chamberlain. The Royal Court (as it has done with plays in more modern times) put the comedy on privately until granted a licence later in the year. As a footnote to the Edwardian theatre it is worth noting that (however fleetingly) Ibsen and Chekhov showed their heads for a few London performances around the turn of the century.

The music hall had a wider popularity than the straight theatre and this was a period when the audiences were so large that performances were given twice-nightly. Exact numbers cannot be calculated, but there were at least 30 music halls in central London and about the same number in the suburbs. The Moss 'Empires' (managed by H.E. Moss and Oswald Stoll) were the opulent leviathans from Shepherd's Bush to Hackney; there were 'Hippodromes' from Putney to Lewisham, with the largest at Lewisham seating over 3,000; 'Palaces' were to be found from Hammersmith to Camberwell. With so many theatres, finding good acts was sometimes a problem. A favourite like Robey would have a cab waiting at the stage door so that he could get round to play five 'dates' in a night.

By the new century the old-time chairman with a gavel announcing 'A big welcome please for…' had all but disappeared, replaced by numbers picked out in electric bulbs on either side of the proscenium. Broad humour and dramatic melodramas had given way to ballets and stately sopranos. Hard benches were superseded by red-plush tip-up seats. With these changes came a

For nearly 100 years the Egyptian Hall in Piccadilly was constantly on the look out for new sensations. At the turn of the century, before the building was demolished in 1904, early films were presented there as 'Improved Animated Photographs'.

new respectability surprising to those who assume that impropriety was a dominant Edwardian trend. Marie Lloyd might still give a knowing wink when she sang 'A Little of What You Fancy…', and *Poses Plastiques* featuring 'living statues' enticed men's opera glasses, but old-time music hall was being replaced by 'Variety'.

Leading the new trend toward's music hall respectability was Oswald Stoll. Already the partner in a chain of music halls, Stoll in 1902 planned to move the centre of his operations from Cardiff, and open a variety theatre in London unlike anything previously conceived. From personal observation outside Charing Cross Station he came to the conclusion that there was a huge potential audience, largely women from the suburbs, who would welcome a show (the right kind of show) after pottering round the shops. Out of this idea grew the Coliseum.

The vast theatre he planned for St Martin's Lane was aimed at a middle-class audience, some of them women on their own, who would find not only seemly entertainment but home comforts as well. In a first-floor, Conservatory teas were served among palm trees with a ladies' orchestra playing. There was a 'Ladies Boudoir' and an 'Information Bureau'; shorthand typists took messages; telegrams could be sent, stamps bought. There were four performances a day (the first at midday) and a stage with three revolving platforms allowed every sort of spectacle including a Roman chariot race and the finale of the Derby with six live horses and jockeys.

After initial excitement and success, the Coliseum lost popularity and in 1906 was closed for 18 months. But Stoll was not beaten. He reopened without resorting to spectacle (except for three elephants playing cricket). He induced a reluctant Sarah Bernhardt to be part of a variety bill, and sticking rigidly to his instructions to artists ('Coarseness and vulgarity are not allowed at the Coliseum') he won success. Although the first Royal Command Variety Performance for George V in 1912 was staged at the Palace and not his Coliseum, the honour drew from Stoll the exclamation: 'The Cinderella of the Arts is going to the ball at last.'

The music hall was so popular that it seemed impossible that it would ever be challenged. But within a few years the cinema began to seduce audiences away from variety. The change began innocently enough with newsreels and comic shorts being introduced into variety bills. The Empire in Leicester Square made a newsreel *London Day by Day* a regular part of its programme with big events like the Derby reaching the screen the following day. Before long the novelty had won sufficient popularity for buildings to be converted into small 'flea pit' cinemas. In Victoria some shops were turned into the Bioscope cinema about 1905; the Balham Empire went over from variety to films in 1909; and soon there were 300 purpose-built cinemas in London.

As early as 1903 the classic American film *The Great Train Robbery* drew excited audiences, and during the next decade Britain developed a small industry of its own, with one pioneer making films at his outdoor studio at Loughborough Junction, which he screened at the Daily Bioscope, a shop converted to hold audiences of a hundred in Bishopsgate. Stage actors were mildly contemptuous but fascinated by the new medium, and soon Henry Ainley and Cyril Maude were working for the London Film Company, which shot pictures at Twickenham and screened them on their own cinema circuit. Godfrey Tearle filmed *Romeo and Juliet* in 1908, and in 1913 (the year he was knighted) Forbes-Robertson made *Hamlet* at Walton-on-Thames.

Before radio, long before television, and with the cinema still in its infancy, reading was the dominant pastime and books, as the poker-work motto proclaimed, were 'silent friends'. With the Education Act of 1902 pushing forward literacy there was more and more call on the 400 public libraries, many founded by the Scottish-born American industrialist Andrew Carnegie, that were open by 1910. For the better-off, private circulating libraries were in constant use and the influence of the most famous — Mudie's in Oxford Street, the City and the West End —

Varied pleasures of Edwardian London are advertised on a poster hoarding in Gerridge Street off Westminster Bridge Road in 1907.

The Russian ballet was in London in 1912 when Tamara Karsavina and Adolph Bolm danced in *The Firebird* at Covent Garden.

may be seen from their catalogues and delivery services. Deliveries went out by motor van to every main suburb in a twenty-mile radius and two or three books were supplied weekly at an annual cost of £1 15s.

The annual additions to Mudie's catalogue show titles produced during the Edwardian decade that made good popular reading. In Diamond Jubilee year H.G. Wells published *The Invisible Man* (1897), and the following appeared, one each year, from the start of the century: Joseph Conrad's *Lord Jim* (1900); Rudyard Kipling's *Kim* (1901); Arthur Conan Doyle's *The Hound of the Baskervilles* (1902); Samuel Butler's *The Way of All Flesh* (1903); Arnold Bennett's *Anna of the Five Towns* (1904); Baroness Orczy's *The Scarlet Pimpernel* (1905); John Galsworthy's *The Man of Property* (1906); Edmund Gosse's *Father and Son* (1907); G.K. Chesterton's *The Man Who Was Thursday* (1908); John Buchan's *Prester John* (1909); E.M. Forster's *Howards End* (1910); Edgar Wallace's *Sanders of the River* (1911); E.C. Bentley's *Trent's Last Case* (1912); D.H. Lawrence's *Sons and Lovers* (1913); Edgar Rice Burroughs's *Tarzan of the Apes* (1914). They may not be 'great literature' or many of them books likely to have been praised by 'the Bloomsbury set' in Gordon Square, but an astonishing number have won immortality.

Because of his death (in May 1910) Edward VII missed two artistic events generally thought of as part of the Edwardian age. He would have been unlikely to have gone anywhere near the Grafton Galleries where the Post-Impressionist exhibition was seen in November but he would have greatly savoured the Russian ballet the following June.

The exhibition that caused the conventional art world to dissolve into hysterics came about by chance; it was a stop-gap show of modern foreign artists which the critic and art pundit Roger Fry got together in a hurry and improvised the name saying 'Oh, let's just call them Post-Impressionists; at any rate, they came after the Impressionists…' So were assembled the first works most Londoners had seen of Cézanne, Matisse, Van Gogh, Gauguin, Seurat and Picasso. Press and public tumbled over each other in noisy execration. Angry exclamations like, 'Pure pornography' were heard. 'Work of idleness and impotent stupidity' was almost a compliment in the chorus of vilification. The whole collection should be burnt, said one critic, and the total value would not be £5. The organiser was spoken of as a charlatan and maniac who should be boycotted by decent society. These were insults that Fry took calmly. He could afford to do so; the Post-Impressionists had given him fame.

Although he did not live to see the full Russian ballet in London, Edward VII could have watched several of the leading dancers. Writers on ballet generally ascribe June 1911 (in the Coronation Season of George V at Covent Garden) as the date when Diaghilev's Ballets Russes first appeared in London, but in fact two years earlier Stoll had been to Russia and brought Tamara Karsavina and ten dancers from St Petersburg to the Coliseum. The King could also have seen Pavlova at the Palace and other Russian dancers such as Lydia Kyasht as guest artists at the Empire or Alhambra. It was left to London in the new reign to relish the exotic *Shéhérazade*, Nijinsky's famous leap in *Le Spectre de la Rose* and the other triumphs briefly enjoyed by Diaghilev's company before the Great War.

After difficult early years, Queen's Hall, Langham
Place, (built 1893, bombed 1941) became an
important centre of London's musical life from early in
the new century. Many of the 2,500 seats were
removed, so doubling the standing room for which one
shilling was charged. Here, audiences at Edwardian
Promenade Concerts responded enthusiastically to the
showmanship of the ebullient conductor Henry Wood
who was knighted in 1911.

Sir Edward Elgar, whose *Pomp and Circumstance*, March No. 1, was a triumphant success at the 'Proms' in 1901, making the first recording of *Carissima* at the Gramophone Company Studio at Hayes in 1914. Elgar wrote the 'Coronation Ode' for Edward VII's Coronation and his Symphony in A Flat in 1908 was widely regarded and heralded as a composition in praise of the Edwardian era.

In 1905, three years after Horseless Carriages were
permitted to travel at 20 m.p.h., Olympia staged its
first Motor show. In 1912 there were 30 stands like
those here with the 'Humberette' offered 'complete
with hood, screen, horn, headlights and taillamps' for
£125. Persuasive salesmen promised a year's 5000-
miles of motoring for £30. With photographs
appearing of King Edward proudly driving a Daimler,
the actress Elizabeth Jay in a sports model (*opposite, top*)
and even a dog called Rover at a steering wheel in a
film comedy (*opposite, bottom*), they had receptive
listeners. By 1914 132,000 private cars were
registered for road use.

Sarah Bernhardt played Hamlet in London and was
lured by Oswald Stoll to the Coliseum for £1,000 a
week, which was paid to her in gold each night before
the performance. When first approached, she
misinterpreted the nature of the Coliseum and is said
to have cabled back: 'After monkeys not'. But she
came in 1910 and three following years.

Ellen Terry, the most famous of the theatrical Terry family, was Henry Irving's leading lady at the Lyceum. She celebrated her stage jubilee in 1906 with a great matinee at Drury Lane when 24 of her family and the most distinguished stage personalities of the day appeared.

The Empire Theatre, Leicester Square, was a
music hall with a raffish reputation and the
Promenade behind the stalls was so notorious
that it caused protests from moral reformers.
People were slightly shocked when Edward VII
made a private visit in 1909. At his Coronation in
1902 the outside was lavishly garlanded and, as
the photograph shows, the Empire staged a
patriotic production entitled *Our Crown*.

George Robey (*above*) who billed himself as the 'Prime Minister of Mirth' was in great demand round the music halls of the period. Marie Lloyd (*right*) was another favourite. Because of touches of vulgarity, Oswald Stoll did not include her in the 1912 Royal Command Variety Performance. To this rebuff she responded by a poster saying 'Every performance by Marie Lloyd is a performance by Command of the British Public'.

Suitably frenetic dancing by Ethel Levey in *Hello Rag-Time!* the American-style revue that caught the spirit of the age at the Hippodrome in 1912.

Carte-de-visite of Edna May the American actress who after her triumph in *The Belle of New York* at the turn of the century, remained in London to score further successes in such musicals as *The School Girl* and *The Catch of the Season*.

Opposite Prestige was given to variety by the Victoria Palace built in 1911 which replaced a tavern music hall. On the dome was placed a statue of Anna Pavlova. Either in silent protest, or out of superstition, the ballerina is said to have always pulled down her car blinds as she passed. *Above* She was less inhibited when she danced (with Laurent Novikoff) for her guests at the garden party at Ivy House, her Hampstead home, in 1912. Her statue on the dome, removed (for safe-keeping) during World War Two, has disappeared.

Dances and balls with their rigid protocol and evening dress began to give way to more informal dances in the new century. The cheek-to-cheek Bunny-Hug and the exotic tango from Argentina became acceptable if, as here at a *thé dansant* in 1914, cups of tea were passed round at the same time.

The Crystal Palace, mid 1890s. Designed by Sir
Joseph Paxton to house the Great Exhibition in Hyde
Park in 1851, it was moved to Sydenham in 1852-4.
Until its destruction by fire in 1936 it proved a popular
setting for a day out.

Enjoying carefree pleasure, 50 or more passengers
weigh down this strange vessel. They are making a trip
round the boating lake of the Crystal Palace in about
1909. After more than half a century of attracting
crowds of visitors Sydenham fell on hard times at this
date and, to avoid bankruptcy, tried various features to
restore its fortunes. This included a folksy lagoon and
bridge with a watershoot.

Pearly quartette. Singing to raise money for charity,
four Pearly Queens parade in all their splendour.
Pearly Kings and Queens, the élite among
costermongers, originally organised themselves for
protection against unscrupulous street traders.
Their pearl-studded costumes are home made in keen
competition, and the best dressed were elected 'King'
or 'Queen' for their particular district each year. In
1911 they formed themselves into a charity-raising
organisation. Up to 1914 London's pavements
swarmed with curbside vendors like the one on the
right selling 'Diabolo', an Edwardian craze. Further
right, a street entertainer in black-face performs in the
hope of a few coins.

OXFORD, 1911.

'In 1906 the Boat Race was still a National Institution. Every cab driver in London tied a dark – or light – blue bow to his whip, every child wore a favour.' So recalled an Oxford President of Boats of the enthusiasm during Edward VII's reign when Oxford won five times and Cambridge four. A photographer, right, before the 1911 boatrace (won by Oxford) catches the crew on the river at Putney.

Right 'Pauline', enigmatically described as Oxford's mascot, who was never far from boathouse or tow path.

Up for the Cup. In 1906 soccer fans arrived in
London sporting favours and carrying rattles to watch
Everton beat Newcastle United one-nil. By Edwardian
times Football League had become a predominantly
professional sport with a large number of northern
sides among Cup Finalists. As many as 120,000
supporters came to cheer their teams at the Crystal
Palace.

Spectators arriving at Wimbledon for the finals in July 1914.

The stands round the Centre Court may have been smaller and long white trousers *de rigueur* for men in this 1909 foursome, but then, as now, the name Wimbledon meant tennis. Championships were played in Worple Road until moving to present Church Road in 1922.

With her strong chin and feared forehand drive Mrs Lambert Chambers battered her way through the Wimbledon singles to win the championship seven times between 1903 and 1914. Vicar's daughter and wife of an Ealing businessman, she could not defend her title in two of those years because she was having babies. Here in 1914, playing in furnace conditions, she won by two straight sets. Only in later years did Mrs Chambers open her blouse at the neck and slightly shorten her skirt.

Two contrasting Edwardian artists. 'A legend. . .the
great artist, the great lover, the great Bohemian' was
how Augustus John (*above*) aged 24 in 1902 was
described by John Rothenstein, future director of the
Tate Gallery. After studying at the Slade, and holding
his first one-man exhibition in his teens, John
preferred a wandering gypsy life. He was in complete
contrast to an older 'establishment' figure of the
period, Sir Alfred East. Seen right, working on one of
the fine landscapes that made him famous, East was
President of the Royal Society of British artists,
knighted in 1910 and elected R.A. in 1913.

To those in 1901 who thought of art in terms of Bond Street galleries and the newly opened Tate, the Whitechapel Art Gallery was a surprising addition to the London scene. It largely owed its East End existence to the social reformer, the Rev. Samuel Barnett, vicar of nearby St Jude's, whose wife was to found Hampstead Garden Suburb. He introduced good art to Whitechapel through exhibitions and lectures at the end of the previous century. Innovation was matched by the Art Nouveau design by Charles Harrison Townsend. Between square towers (without their planned cupolas) was a space for a (never erected) mosaic by Stephen Crane symbolising the 'Sphere and Message of Art'. Internationally renowned art shows started at Whitechapel with the 1902 Japanese Exhibition. The obelisk outside the gallery brought from the Great Exhibition had no local significance and was demolished in 1913.

Next door to the Whitechapel Art Gallery was the free
library named after John Passmore Edwards, the
philanthropist who mainly financed the gallery and
founded the library. Increased literacy around the turn
of the century led to the opening of many public
libraries. Paid for from the rates, this one at Westfield
House, Fulham, in about 1908 installed electricity and
especially catered for readers' interest in newspapers.
Other free libraries in Britain came into being thanks
to Andrew Carnegie, the Scottish-born American
industrialist, who financed the building of 380
libraries, many of them in London.

Four of the most successful men in the Edwardian theatre. After *The Admirable Crichton* (1902) James Barrie (*far left*) had a new play in London nearly every year until 1913. The others talking to Harley Granville-Barker (*far right*) are John Galsworthy, and next to Granville-Barker, Bernard Shaw, both of whom wrote plays for the playwright-actor-producer's outstanding regime at the Royal Court Theatre.

In May 1912 a statue of Peter Pan appeared suddenly
in Kensington Gardens. Nina Boucicault, the boy who
never grew up in the original 1904 production of
James Barrie's play, was the model for the sculptor Sir
George Frampton. Barrie employed workmen and the
statue was erected literally overnight so that children
would think that it had been put there by fairies. This
whimsical idea led to a Question in the House—
should a private person be allowed to erect a statue in
a public park?—when it was discovered that the
Commissioner of Works had been party to the plan.

The Edwardian literary scene saw fame for writers as
diverse as Max Beerbohm (*above*), the elegant essayist
whose Oxford fantasy *Zuleika Dobson* delighted readers
in 1911; Arthur Conan Doyle (*opposite, top*), creator of
such Sherlock Holmes stories as *The Hound of the
Baskervilles* (1902); Virginia Woolf (*opposite, below*), a
leader of the future 'Bloomsbury Group', with her
father Sir Leslie Stephen on whom the character of
Mr Ramsey in her *To The Lighthouse* is reputedly based.
Sir Leslie was editor of the *Dictionary of National
Biography* and an author, the last of whose many books
was published on the day of his death in 1904.

On a summer's day in 1909 a sense of unexplained expectancy hangs over London Bridge. There is no clue as to why the crowd, almost entirely men, are peering over the parapets. Horse-drawn vehicles and a man pushing a safety bicycle make up the traffic, while in front of the columned Customs House a popular Thames Steamer carries passengers down river.

HALE'S STORES.

From the time when films were first shown using a hand-cranked projector in an improvised hall, some 300 cinemas had been specially built by 1910. Many of them had the assumed dignity of the Old Ford Picture Palace in north-east London (*above*), whose manager wore a top hat and a dinner jacket. With the outbreak of the Great War the Cinematograph Theatre, Edgware Road (*opposite*), proclaimed 'This cinema is owned and controlled by Englishmen.'

In the age when travel relied almost entirely on trains, large trunks and heavy luggage on the platform at Paddington in 1911 are ready to be put aboard a boat train. Less ambitiously, a little family have their bits and pieces, a strapped wicker case and a bicycle, before leaving Waterloo for a holiday on the south coast.

CHAPTER SIX

Age of Unrest and Reform

The public and press hardly noticed a meeting that took place near Ludgate Circus in February 1900. They were preoccupied by the headline news that in South Africa Ladysmith had been relieved after a 118-day siege. But the assembly at the Memorial Hall, Farringdon Street, was of more than slight importance. It marked the birth of the Labour Party.

After a day-long debate delegates from 65 trade unions and three Socialist societies passed a resolution to establish 'a distinct Labour Group in Parliament'. They represented 568,000 workers; there was some split among the rival factions in the hall; their secretary was Ramsay MacDonald, the future Prime Minister. Even if the proposals made were not very revolutionary, the occasion was a sufficient break-through for Keir Hardie, Scottish miner and Labour leader, to indulge in a rhetorical flourish. Greeting the Labour Party, he said: 'It has come! Poor little child of danger, nursling of the storm. May it be blessed.' The delegates walked out into the rain and into a new century of change.

Having established a political bridgehead unions were relatively quiet for the next few years. Such as they were, strikes between 1901 and 1907 were limited in size but variations in industrial action were not a true barometer of prevailing poverty and social inequality. For that we must look to *Life and Labour of the People in London* (revised in 1903) in which Charles Booth depicted over 30 per cent of the population living in poverty and conditions of particular squalour existing in the Shadwell, Limehouse, Stepney and Whitechapel areas of the East End.

Booth's famous 'poverty map' graphically showed the division between 70 per cent rich and 30 per cent poor marked by Regent Street, which with its affluent shops separated Mayfair from the slums round Seven Dials, where whole families lived on as little as 18 shillings a week. The Victorian radical John Bright found a term for persons of 'almost helpless poverty and dependence'; he called them 'the residium' of society. Another Booth, William Booth, founder of the Salvation Army, described them as 'the submerged tenth'.

Help for the poor was sporadic at best. In 1902 the London County Council (which by then had been in existence for 14 years) looked at unemployment and could only suggest that boroughs set up 'schemes of public work'. Charity organisations opened 'Winter Distress Funds' but these were badly conducted. Social observers talked ominously of the cauldron of despair boiling over.

Poverty in London was increased to some degree by the number of immigrants who, thanks to tolerant legislation, were permitted into the country. This greatly helped people suffering from political and religious persecution and contrasted with the United States, where restrictions were imposed in the 1880s. Generally arriving at the London docks from the Continent,

A Suffragette escorted by police from Buckingham Palace. The women's movement increasingly made the palace a focus for their assaults to gain the maximum of publicity.

the immigrants moved into the East End where many were employed in the lowest forms of manual labour. By 1901 there were 42,000 Russians and Poles living in Stepney. The competition caused by these and other foreigners (they worked 18-hour days for bare wages) was naturally resented.

Conditions were harsh for new arrivals but the influx from Europe gave the East End a cosmopolitan flavour, which it has never completely lost. The members of the European community were adept at making themselves at home. Early in the century Russians had established a free library of their own in Church Lane off the Commercial Road and the Ghetto Bank in Whitechapel to send home what money they could afford to their relatives.

Limehouse became a convenient place for Chinese seamen and ships' launderers to settle. Fiction spread a lurid picture of opium dens, but a greater and more practical reality was a mission house run by a clergyman who had spent much of his earlier working life in China. Each July 'Little Italy' celebrated the 'Festival of the Madonna' with a two-mile procession through the East End streets. German settlers, many of them prosperous, not only opened a lager beer saloon in Glasshouse Street near Piccadilly Circus, but were sufficiently influential to publish their own newspaper *Londoner Zeitung* and open a hospital for their compatriots in Dalston.

The British Isles made their own contribution to local colour. In London this was helped by the Gaelic League, which kept Irish traditions alive in what is now John Adam Street in the Adelphi area, where it was a rule that only Gaelic should be spoken. The Welsh could claim a

Until social reform came about through legislation, help for the poor mostly took the form of charity. These men in 1907 are being given a free meal after taking part in a religious service.

50,000 London community, and London's Scots clung to their native accents (and celebrated Burns Night with fervour) at the Caledonian Club off St James's. Membership of a Wimbledon golf club also demanded north of the border affiliations.

Extreme poverty had somehow to be overcome and the destitute, tramps, and 'unemploy-ables' given help. A practical solution came from Winston Churchill at the Board of Trade in 1909. He pressed for 'labour exchanges', places where the 'irretrievable poor' would be treated not as social outcasts but more as if they were hospital patients. The name arose because it was hoped that these would be places where jobs would be 'exchanged' for unemployment.

A 'Social Service State' had a ring of anarchy to many in Edwardian society, but in 1902 the first important measure was taken with the introduction of the Education Act by A.J. Balfour's Conservative government when for the first time secondary education became a responsibility of the State. With the Liberal landslide in 1906 came the Trades Disputes Acts, which meant that unions were exempted from legal actions resulting from damage during strikes.

A whole series of Liberal reforms during the premiership of H.H. Asquith followed until 1914. By far the most popular Act of Parliament brought the granting of old age pensions in 1909, which the elderly were able to draw at post offices. Two men of very different back-grounds, Lloyd George, Chancellor of the Exchequer, and Winston Churchill at the Board of Trade, prepared new schemes for health and unemployment. The Children's Act curbed mal-treatment, and the Housing and Town Planning Act gave local authorities the power to clear slums and prohibit the building of back-to-back houses. It was also in 1909 that two great reformers, Sidney and Beatrice Webb, drawing on middle-class support for their Fabian Society, recruited 25,000 members to serve on their Prevention of Destitution Committee.

These reforms showed a great advance in enlightened thinking, and the treatment of people under the Poor Law changed from being a charity into a right. Until then the increase in hospi-tal attendances (inevitable with the growth of population) were often put down to 'imaginary ailments'. Even a reasonably enlightened social worker could write: 'hundreds of poor women are tempted to live on drugs, tonics and cordials to the neglect of the real source of health — reg-ular employment, good food, cleanliness and roomy well-ventilated dwellings'. He failed to explain how the poor would be able to obtain these panaceas.

This attitude was in line with arguments put forward by a section of society which believed in the doctrine that people were best helped by helping themselves. It was the kind of thinking that brought about one extraordinary reaction to the National Insurance Act of 1911. By this law employers were to provide stamps for their servants' cards so that they could draw benefit in case of sickness. It would have seemed an enlightened enough plan, but led to 'two ladies of title' organising a mass meeting of servants and their mistresses at the Albert Hall. A 'noble chair-woman' contended that sticking on insurance stamps would 'ruin the beautiful intimacy which has hitherto so often existed between mistresses and servants'. Reports do not say if any cynically minded servant raised the point that there was a greater danger that a tight-fisted employer might deduct the cost of the stamp from wages.

So mild a domestic wrangle seems historically trivial when set against unrest, foreign in ori-gin, that took place in 1907. The Fifth Congress of the Russian Social Democratic Party was held in — of all places — Islington. There is no record that it planned to undermine Britain, but among the 336 delegates were Lenin, Stalin (under the alias of Koba-Ivanovich), Trotsky, Gorky and the German revolutionary Rosa Luxemburg. When the name of Litvinov, Lenin's future Commissar for Foreign Affairs, is added, and the place of the meeting noted (the Brotherhood Chapel, Southgate Road) a stranger cast and an odder setting for the fermentation of an epic revolution would be hard to imagine.

The red bogey was revived three years later by a different, more overtly violent event when a group of Russian-speaking anarchists held out against soldiers and 400 armed police in the Siege of Sidney Street. The mysterious ringleader 'Peter the Painter' disappeared (leading to the totally unfounded legend that he was Lenin) and Winston Churchill, by then Home Secretary, made a visit to the scene, which he left after three hours giving the impression that he had cleared up all the trouble.

The opening six years of Edward VII's reign were free of serious industrial stoppages, and the first major confrontation came after his death. A short-lived, two-day rail strike in August 1911 was a small rumble before a storm that same summer when 100,000 dockers and seamen marched through the City to Tower Hill and Trafalgar Square and were faced with the threat of soldiers being brought in to unload ships. The following year saw a further dock strike in which strikers went back after ten weeks of hardship. Blacklegs had weakened their position and from then on workers saw solidarity as essential. In any one industry strikers found that they generally lacked strength but plans for a triple alliance (port workers uniting with railway-men and miners) went into abeyance with the outbreak of the Great War.

The Great War was to delay another cause. Of all the political agitation identified with Edwardian London, the Suffragette movement is now recalled with something near incredulity. The fanatical dedication with which the campaign was fought over a period of ten years wins admiration but also explains why some excesses caused antagonism.

During the 1912 Transport Strike East End workers try to stop an insulated van probably containing meat. A policeman struggles with a jammed wheel and other police are on duty with orders to get the delivery through.

The imprisonment of women, their hunger strikes and forcible feeding followed with increasing intensity from 1903 when Mrs Emmeline Pankhurst from Manchester started the suffragettes (properly the Women's Social and Political Union) and established their headquarters in Clifford's Inn. The proximity to Fleet Street, it was correctly thought, would help publicity. The movement need not have spread if a bill to give women the vote had not been 'talked out' in the House by an M.P. who informed members that 'men and women differ in mental equipment with women having little sense'. They were too passionate and unbalanced for political life; giving them the vote, he said, would not be safe.

Such an inflammatory speech made suffragettes deaf to the advice of the Prime Minister, Sir Henry Campbell-Bannerman, who said that women would be far more likely to succeed if they did not show a pugnacious attitude. How his advice was ignored is history that sometimes reads like melodrama.

In the decade leading up to the Great War the catalogue of violence varied from the courageous to the seemingly paranoid. Routine violence embraced damage to West End stores by shattering windows with stones and hammers concealed in muffs and setting Westminster pillar boxes on fire with rags dipped in paraffin. The greens of golf clubs were burned with acid. The Orchid House and Tea Pavilion at Kew were wrecked. A country railway station was burned down. Both Lloyd George and Churchill were assailed: Lloyd George the more seriously when a bomb was placed in the bedroom of his house at Walton Heath, Churchill when assaulted on Bristol railway station by a woman with a dog whip. Faintly comical and *outré* was the Suffragette daughter of an actor who attacked windows of Victoria Street shops with a catapult from the top of a bus. Before a large Hyde Park rally M.P.s on the terrace of the House were taunted by a leading militant who hired a launch and shouted across the water through a microphone: 'Come to the Park on Sunday. There will be no arrests — you shall have plenty of police protection!'

Over the years women's suffrage was debated more than 50 times by Parliament, and particular resentment followed the treatment of a Bill in 1908. The Bill which would have given the vote to every woman with household qualifications received 299 votes on the first reading but the Government blocked further progress because of 189 against. Frustrations of this sort increased militancy, which had its horrific climax when Emily Davison, an Oxford Honours graduate, ran onto the course during the 1913 Derby and was killed by the king's horse. A few months later a journalist of 31, Mary Richardson, went to the National Gallery and slashed a painting by Velasquez with a chopper. The damage (successfully repaired) was set at £40,000. She received a six-month sentence.

When he succeeded his father George V found himself personally involved in the conflict when a kneeling debutante at a Palace presentation looked up and said: 'Your Majesty, stop forcible feeding!' His reply is not recorded, but later his confused reaction was: 'I don't know what we are coming to!'

What the country was coming to was the Great War, which was to bring an end to the 11 years of seemingly insoluble deadlock. Within a month of war being declared the Suffragettes suspended all activities and those imprisoned were released. In 1917 the vote was given to all women over 30 and this was reduced to 21 (the same age as men) within a few years. It was a long overdue victory for the Suffragettes and one which some male reactionaries conceded only grudgingly. They continued to insist that women had no inherent right to the vote but said they should be awarded it for their splendid war service.

Above The poverty-stricken neighbourhood of Stepney provided a wretched kitchen for a woman and her children. The date and exact whereabouts are not known.

Left Nowhere is hoplessness more evident than in Providence Place, Stepney, which was in every sense a blind alley for those seen standing by their doorways in 1908. Narrow courtyards like this and so-called rookeries were off Middlesex Street ('Petticoat Lane') near Whitechapel High Street. Providence Place was demolished within a few years of this picture being taken.

Ragged children taking advantage of a Poplar
watercart in 1910 provide a welcome sidelight to the
grim poverty statistics. 'Caution Poison' on the side of
the cart would be a warning against water being
collected for drinking.

Escaping from foreign pogroms, Jews arrived in their
thousands from Europe. They set up many bakeries of
their own and here, probably in Poplar, a special loaf
arriving in a cart is the focus for the children's interest.

In the groves of Edwardian academe. A gramophone is brought to the aid of a French master at Westminster School in 1909 (*opposite, top*). His class is perceptibly smaller than the one of science at Friern secondary school (*above*) about the same year. In the new century higher education for women in London was well established with Bedford College in Regent's Park and Royal Holloway College. Although at Egham, Surrey, Holloway became a school of London University in 1900 with an intake of about 50 arts and science students a year. Tea and a fry-up in a comfortable room appears to have been part of their amenities (*opposite, bottom*).

Opposite East End social work included meagre but
welcome meals known as 'farthing breakfasts'.

Bathing of a rather primitive sort was provided by this
'Cleansing Station' in Stepney. Children came to this
centre in Finch Street (now Hopetown Street) for the
removal of lice and to be given baths not available in
their homes.

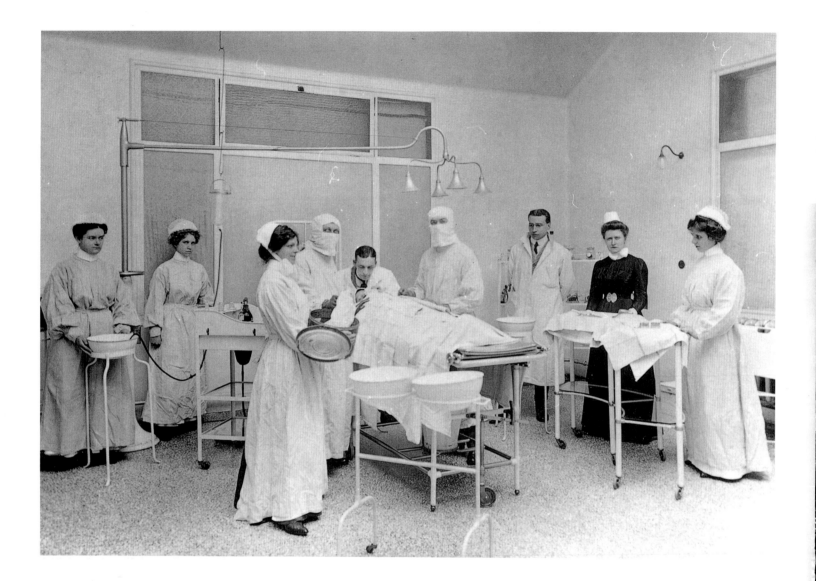

Most of the famous London hospitals were long
established, and, by Edwardian times, to these were
added poor law infirmaries with trained nurses, which
were supported by the rates and charity. Treatment
was mostly for chronic rather than acute illnesses. The
operating theatre at Fulham Union Infirmary prided
itself on carrying out as many as 200 operations a year
by 1910 in a 'pavilion' equipped with anaesthetising
and sterilising rooms.

A team of midwives stand at the alert. Midwives and maternity care became more widely available once Lloyd George's National Health Insurance Act was introduced in 1911.

Opposite Lloyd George, Chancellor of the Exchequer on his way to the House to present his 1910 Budget with Winston Churchill, President of the Board of Trade. Politicians of very different backgrounds—one brought up by a village cobbler, the other a duke's grandson—they formed a friendship and an alliance to bring about social reform. This was under Asquith's Liberal premiership, and Asquith's daughter maintained that Churchill 'was to learn the language of Radicalism' from Lloyd George.

Above In a top hat and fur-collared overcoat Winston Churchill, by then Home Secretary, peers gingerly round a corner during the Siege of Sidney Street off the Mile End Road. For six hours after dawn on 3 January 1911 two armed foreign fugitives kept at bay 400 policemen, a squad of Scots Guards, the Fire Brigade and a detachment of Royal Engineers. 'Why not an airship?' was one satirical comment. Finally, the house caught fire and the pair died in a Wagnerian climax to the siege, which has become part of London folklore as well as making this one of the most famous Press photographs ever taken.

Immigration brought thousands of people from abroad to Britain, many of whom settled in the East End. Entry regulations were liberal and because they represented cheap labour many foreigners were resented. These two neatly dressed Chinese youths in a Limehouse café (*right*) show no sign of being opium fiends or the sort of villains portrayed by Sax Rohmer in his 1913 novel *Dr Fu Manchu*.

Opposite Russians sought refuge in Britain and, like so many foreigners, tried to preserve their native pleasures. The design and pretensions of the Russian Vapour Bath in Brick Lane, Stepney, indicate that it enjoyed considerable local patronage.

Below The camera caught this informal Italian family group in 1907.

Unemployment (then a new word in the language) described by Winston Churchill, the Trade Minister, as 'the problem of the hour,' provoked unrest and this protest march in Trafalgar Square in 1908 (*left*). The Labour Party tried unsuccessfully to force a 'Bill of Right to Work' through Parliament. Edwardian statistics are too sketchy to be comprehensive but in one of the worst years, such as 1908, a national total of 1,450,000 were out of work. Taking temporary measures to stem the tide, the War Office recruited 24,000 Reserves, the Post Office took on 8,000 and the Admiralty brought 2,100 workers into the dockyards.

Above The men in cloth caps and mufflers are part of a dole queue in 1911 in the dejected East End of London.

Ben Tillett, Labour Leader from Bristol who started
his working life in a brickworks, addressing strikers in
1911. An early organiser of the Dockers Union, he
formed the National Transport Workers Federation
and was to become a Labour M.P.

John Burns, the militant labour politician known as 'The man with the Red Flag' (because he carried the traditional symbol of radicalism at his open-air meetings), addressing voters at Battersea in 1910. By this date, and having represented Battersea since 1906, Burns had modified his radicalism to stand, and be re-elected, as a Liberal.

An omnibus covered in notices travelled through the
West End in October 1909 to advertise a new issue of
the Suffragette newspaper *Votes for Women*.

Backed by her mother, Christabel Pankhurst making one of the Trafalgar Square speeches in October 1908 that led to their arrest, court appearance and subsequent imprisonment on the grounds that they were exhorting people to help the Suffragettes 'rush' the House of Commons.

Left Christabel and Emmeline Pankhurst with Flora Drummond between them at Bow Street following the Trafalgar Square meeting. They were accused of 'conduct likely to cause a breach of the peace.' Christabel delivered a very long speech challenging evidence given by the Chancellor of the Exchequer, Lloyd George. At the hearing Max Beerbohm, drama critic turned court reporter for a day, wrote: 'As she stood there, with her head held merrily to one side, trilling her answers to the Chancellor of the Exchequer, she was like nothing so much as a little singing bird born in captivity.'

CHAPTER SEVEN
'Georgian' Epilogue

Edward VII's reign of nine years and three and a half months ended a few minutes before midnight on 6 May 1910. He was 68. Except to his doctors and family his sudden death from bronchitis and a heart attack was unexpected. On the morning of his death he met family and friends as cheerfully as possible. When told that one of his horses had won at Kempton Park that afternoon he managed a smile and said 'I am glad.' Among his last reported words before losing consciousness and being carried to bed, 'I shall work to the end', were particularly recalled by those anxious to dispel the image of an unduly frivolous king.

As his most enduring and loving mistress, Mrs Keppel naturally wished to be at his bedside. This outweighed any question of propriety, and Queen Alexandra magnanimously invited her to come to the Palace, which she did on the night of his death or the morning after.

In one respect Edward had made preparations for his death more thoroughly than Victoria. He had always been shocked how little time had been allowed for the nation to pay respects to his mother. To prevent this recurring he left orders that his body was to be laid out in his bedroom and photographed before being put in an oak coffin in the throne room of Buckingham Palace, where it could be visited by relatives and close friends.

After two days at Buckingham Palace the coffin was taken on a gun carriage to Westminster Hall and placed on a catafalque with, around it, four gentlemen-at-arms, heads bowed and arms reversed. During the next three days a quarter of a million members of the public queued to file past the body.

The two weeks between King Edward's death and the funeral allowed time for the arrival of what was probably the greatest concourse of foreign royalty and dignitaries ever assembled. With the break-up of Europe following the Great War its equivalent was never to be seen again. As well as nine sovereigns among fifty-eight men of royal rank, there were two important foreign representatives, Stephen Pichon, French Foreign Minister and the former United States President Theodore Roosevelt.

The silent crowds lining the funeral route had only had time to assess in general terms what they thought about their dead king. Certainly he had been a man who embodied many characteristics the country admired: affability, an easy-going way of life, enjoyment of sport and entertainment. His secretary Sir Frederick Ponsonby who knew him better than most, and in all his moods, summed him up as 'a lovable, wayward and human monarch'.

The role of a constitutional monarch in the early twentieth century is not easy to assess. King Edward's supposedly greatest diplomatic success was the *Entente Cordiale* with the French, but his responsibility for the initiation or conclusion of the agreement has been denied by one of

In the throne room of Buckingham Palace Edward's coffin bearing the crown and orb was seen by privileged visitors for two days. Officers of the Brigade of Guards stood sentinel with reversed arms.

his biographers and also by A.J. Balfour, Prime Minister at the time.

Whatever part Edward played, negotiations came at a moment when Anglo-French relations were at a very low ebb and the need for an *entente* was mainly fostered by the threat of German aggression. The lead-up to the signing of the agreement in April 1904 involved a year of red-carpet exchanges during which Edward visited Paris, incognito but highly visible at the opera, Longchamps races and a garden party at the British Embassy. In return the French President Emile Loubet came to England and agreement was reached. However negligible this may have appeared in 1904, its importance was to be seen ten years later. Along with the Triple Alliance with Russia (visited by King Edward in 1908) these, the principal foreign negotiations of his reign, were to decide Britain's role when the Great War came.

Loved, but a good deal of an enigma, Edward came to final rest when his coffin was lowered into the royal tombhouse under St George's Chapel, Windsor. It had been a long day and one filled with emotion and spectacle; so filled, that it gave one little girl an excuse for not saying her prayers. 'It won't be any use,' decided the child reviewing the occasion, 'God will be too busy unpacking King Edward.'

A little over four years separated the funeral from 1914, the date that it seems appropriate to regard as the end of the Edwardian era. Nearing 45 when he came to the throne, George V had many of his father's problems to deal with, but before he fully took over the reins he visited India, where he was created King Emperor at the Delhi Durbar.

He came back to a country faced with constitutional problems. The House of Lords was rejecting an increase in old age pensions; there was a threat of civil war in Ireland over Home Rule; stepping up their aggression, suffragettes were creating serious damage in the West End;

After his appointment as first lord of the Admiralty in October 1911, Winston Churchill goes to Buckingham Palace to see the new king.

the worst transport strike of the century was about to take place. These were matters uncongenial to a sailor king who, in many ways like his father, enjoyed racing and sporting events. His preferences were for such simple pleasures as a morning canter in Rotten Row and an evening at home with his stamp collection.

Among the things that Edward VII had planned but still remained unfinished at his death was an important project affecting a sensitive part of London. This was a memorial to his mother. An imposing statue was designed, but it was decided that a more comprehensive 'great architectural and scenic change' to the Mall should also be made in her memory.

The memorial cost the then enormous sum of £325,000. The erection of 2,300 tons of marble, starting in 1906, was so large an undertaking that work was still going on in 1911 when the memorial was unveiled and the sculptor, Thomas Brock, knighted on the steps during the ceremony. For some tastes the wealth of allegorical detail is too ornate. There is no compulsion to inspect too closely this 82-feet-high monument crowned by a gilt figure of Victory; it is wiser to see it as part of the larger conception of a ceremonial route.

The Commonwealth contributed large sums for the memorial, which was given a commanding position in front of Buckingham Palace on a *rond point* that was symbolically the hub of the Empire. The designer of the overall plan was Sir Aston Webb and took shape on his drawing board over a decade. Webb had a style that suited Edwardian taste — straightforward with enough ornamentation to be impressive. His scheme extended beyond the memorial to include the Mall, which was widened and laid out with a double avenue of plane trees leading to a monumental entrance, Admiralty Arch, at the far end.

Admiralty Arch was erected to replace a muddle of buildings that had previously impeded access into Trafalgar Square. Curved, massive and consisting of three smaller archways, Admiralty Arch has a carved Latin inscription that gives the date as 1910 although the Arch was only just ready to be used for George V's 1911 coronation.

One last stage was needed in the completion of the grand plan; this was Buckingham Palace, which was in poor shape. The Caen stone that had been used to face the east front in the previous century had weathered badly. Now was the moment to renovate the exterior to provide a fitting backdrop to the Victoria Memorial. Again Aston Webb was ready. He designed a new east facade and the transformation during the late summer of 1913 was something of an engineering feat. It was carried out in only 13 weeks while the royal family was comfortably absent at Balmoral. George V sent down notes and annotated drawings requesting Webb to make sure that the central balcony should 'not be curtailed as it is used from time to time on occasions when the king and other members of the royal family wish to show themselves to the people'.

After the completion of the Palace less than a year remained of the Georgian aftermath to Edwardian tranquillity before the coming of war. Despite labour problems and serious unrest in Ireland for the great majority of people this was an untroubled time which made the sudden appearance of dark clouds over Europe all the more incomprehensible. Statesmen, of course, had long been uneasy, and George V had felt the first premonition of trouble when the Kaiser's brother, Prince Henry of Prussia, visited him at the end of 1912. The German prince asked him point-blank where Britain would stand in the event of Germany going to war against France and Russia. The King replied: 'With the latter.' Again in July 1914 Prince Henry, ostensibly in England on holiday, raised the same question. The King restated his hope that the country would not be drawn into a European conflict. When this was relayed to the Kaiser he is said to have misinterpreted it as a declaration of British neutrality. When reminded that Britain had a treaty upholding Belgium's neutrality he dismissed it as 'a scrap of paper'.

These were among the miscalculations that led up to the 'terrible catastrophe' as the King in his diary described the outbreak of the Great War. Fortunately the country's leaders had not completely lowered their guard; apprehensively watching the European scene they had prepared contingencies for war. Among them was an addition to the Grand Fleet. In the year before Edward VII's death H.M.S. *Thunderer* was laid down at the Thames Ironworks, a shipyard on the north side of the river at Blackwall. At the Admiralty, where he became First Lord that same year, Churchill supervised a huge map on which the movements of the German navy were updated daily. Having had little more than possible trouble in Ireland to worry about, the Army was not so fully prepared. The British Expeditionary Force that went to France in August 1914 consisted of only some 110,00 with a 'sabre strength' of 7,600.

The summer of 1914 was uncommonly hot, but, roused out of lethargy and sweltering temperatures of 90 degrees, London responded to the news of war with enthusiasm. Crowds poured down the Mall on the evening of 4 August and in response to cheering George V came out three times onto the balcony of the Palace — the balcony he had worried about, little envisaging what its first royal use would be. In Downing Street there were more crowds and more cheering, which prompted Sir Edward Grey, looking out of his Foreign Office window, to make an oracular pronouncement to a journalist conveniently present. 'The lamps are going out all over Europe,' he said. 'We shall not see them lit again in our time.'

Events, serious and trivial, followed with painful swiftness. At the Oval it was announced that the Jack Hobbs Benefit Match would be transferred to Lord's; the Army was commandeering the Kennington ground. At Olympia people were less immediately concerned with the war than whether Britain's 'Gunboat' Smith would win the World Heavyweight boxing title. At the Coliseum a Grand Patriotic Chorus of a Hundred Voices was raised in a deafening rendering of *It's a Long Way to Tipperary*, while delivery boys whistled 'Sister Susie's Sewing Socks for Soldiers' from *Hello Rag-Time!* at the Hippodrome.

Posters on London buses showed a heavily moustached General Kitchener pointing his finger with the exhortation, 'Your King and Country Needs You'. At a time long before conscription, Whitehall recruiting offices were inundated with 30,000 volunteers for France; because everyone said it would be 'all over by Christmas', they did not want to miss the fun.

Some alarm was shown by people queuing at the Bank of England to exchange paper money for sovereigns. There was also an outbreak of xenophobia; foreign accents were suspect, and for fear of having their windows stoned, East End shopkeepers put up notices saying they were Russians or other allied immigrants. A German barber in the Caledonian Road was arrested as a spy, and, at a rather different level, Prince Louis of Battenburg (whose son became Lord Louis Mountbatten) resigned as First Sea Lord fearing public reaction to his name, birth and parentage.

Soon realities had to be faced. Men who had left boasting that they would give the Hun a bloody nose were coming back from a little Belgian township named Mons bandaged and with a look of horror in their eyes. Crowds watching Red Cross ambulances turning into Charing Cross Hospital were no longer cheering. On Christmas Eve 1914 a small German biplane came over England, the first air raid in the country's history, and that same night in Flanders Allied and German soldiers ventured out into no-man's-land to sing hymns together and exchange cigarettes. It was a spontaneous gesture; sadly it underlined that the war was not over by Christmas.

Launch of H.M.S. Thunderer

A.H.Judd & Co
Southend-on-Sea.

Spectators cheer as H.M.S *Thunderer* comes down the slipway of a Dagenham shipyard in February 1911. The 22,300 ton battleship was to take part in the Battle of Jutland. She was the last major ship from the Thames Ironworks Yard, which the same year went into liquidation after about 70 years of shipbuilding.

As George V was seen conscientiously touring the battlefields and inspecting the Navy, and with the curtailing of meals at Buckingham Palace, there was speculation about how his father would have responded to the war and faced its austerities. Recalling King Edward's good spirits, George V's secretary, Lord Stamfordham, ventured to ask if his master could look a little more genial during his public appearances to which the king replied: 'We sailors never smile on duty'. King Edward's naturally benign character would have been good for morale but one historian considers that while Edward was a good king for the period in which he lived he would have been both physically uncomfortable and ill at ease in a country at war. With his temperament more suited to pleasure than distress perhaps it was no bad thing that his reign ended and the curtain fell when it did on Edwardian London.

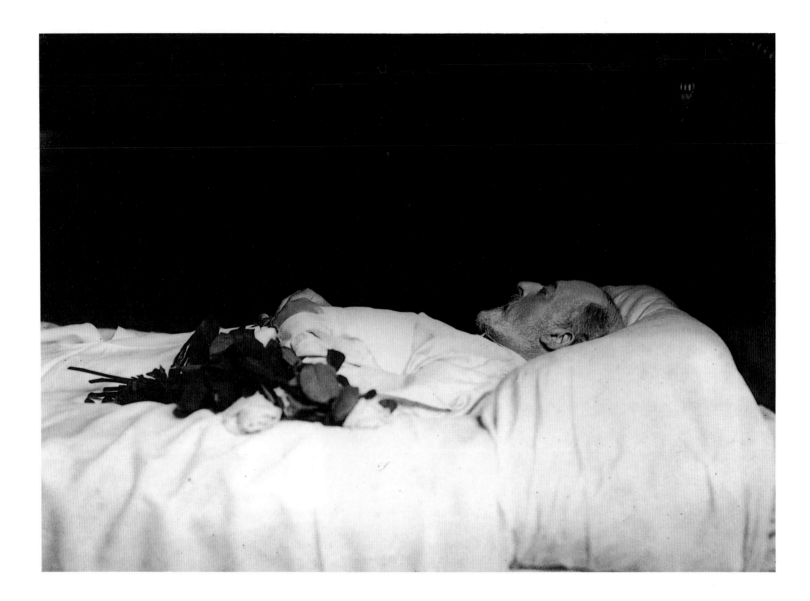

Edward VII on his deathbed. The King's decision to have his picture taken after his death was unprecedented and the photograph of him—eyes closed and at peace—was published to be seen by the whole nation. How this came about is part of Fleet Street legend. A royal photographer was invited to the Palace to take a private picture; the *Daily Mirror* got wind of this and offered him £100. With Queen Alexandra's permission this was accepted and the image appeared under the caption 'White Roses. The Queen Mothers's last tribute of love laid by the side of her dead husband'. It was published twice and the second time, on the morning after the funeral, helped to secure a record newspaper circulation of 2,013,000 copies.

Booted, spurred, with dress swords at their sides and their chests hung with sashes and glittering medals, there is a look of Ruritanian splendour about the nine sovereigns who came to London for the funeral. They are, left to right, standing: King Haakon VII of Norway, Kind Ferdinand of Bulgaria, King Manuel of Portugal, Emperor William II of Germany, King George I of the Hellenes, King Albert of the Belgians. Seated are: King Alfonso XIII of Spain, King George V and King Frederick VIII of Denmark.

The Widow.

The funeral procession from Westminster Hall to Paddington on the way to Windsor. Behind the coffin on a gun-carriage is the Admiral of the Fleet followed by the king's horse with his master's boots reversed in the stirrups. Then, trotting along led by a Highlander, is Edward VII's pet dog, a rough-haired terrier named Caesar. The kaiser further behind is supposed to have complained that never before in his life had be been obliged to yield precedence to a dog. This Germanic joke was to be interpreted as an evil augury in 1914.

Above Waiting for their carriage. A peer and two
guests after George V's Coronation.

Left Police testing the stands for the Coronation.

The Queen Victoria Memorial (*opposite, above*) was unveiled in 1911 but it was to be another three years before the old facade of Buckingham Palace was replaced with the present classical design (*opposite, below*).

Buckingham Palace before its new facade in 1913, seen in the background of the lake in St James's Park.

The most impressive London scheme projected in
Edward VII's reign was the building of Admiralty
Arch and widening of the Mall to make a processional
route to the Victoria Memorial and Buckingham
Palace. Viewed from above Trafalgar Square, in the
foreground is the statue of Charles I, while the
memorial and palace stand at the far end of the Mall.
Breaking the skyline are, right, the Duke of York's
Column and, left, the massive fourteen-storey high
Queen Anne's Mansions (now demolished) in Petty
France with a glimpse of the campanile of
Westminster Cathedral beyond.

Popular reaction to the outbreak of the Great War was not all flag waving and jingoism. Trafalgar Square, traditional forum of revolt, saw peace demonstrations before war fever took a grip. Sitting on the edge of a fountain is Donald Rose, a bearded veteran protester of 88, and lifelong conscientious objector. Arguments are put more dramatically by fervent socialist and Labour M.P. Keir Hardie (*right*). As he did at the time of the Boer War, Hardie speaks out against fighting. Hardie's realisation that working class protest was powerless to prevent war contributed to a breakdown in health. This speech was made in 1914; within a year of the outbreak of war he was dead.

Before it showed itself in all its horrors, the Great War crept up quietly on London. After the declaration of war the removal of the door plate from the German Embassy at 9 Carlton House Terrace tells a clear if undramatic story (*right*).

Below The photograph of a regular soldier in his dress uniform with the caption 'Taking his family for a farewell walk' has a muted, but prophetic irony.

Only with Red Cross ambulances arriving at Charing
Cross Hospital in 1914 does the full message strike
home.

Picture Credits

Thanks are given for kind permission from Her Majesty the Queen to publish photographs from the Royal Collection and to those in charge of public archives, private collections and photographic agencies. Everything has been done to ensure accuracy in captioning, and we hope there are no mistakes or wrong attributions. Describing illustrations has not always been easy and we have often had to rely on interpretation of internal features to settle on dates and decide details of topography.

Aerofilms of Borehamwood (Mills Collection):138; 139

Britsh Film Institute: 156

By permission of the British Library (Shelfmark 201 (b)): 29

The Elgar Foundation: 125

Elmbridge Museum: 127 bottom

Fotomas Index: 119

Greater London Photograph Library: 82; 83; 84; 85 top; 90-91; 92; 109; 120; 166; 168; 170; 173; 179

Guildhall Library, Corporation of London: 18-19; 76; 86-7; 141 left; 162 (*F.G. Hodsoll*); 191; 194; 199 bottom; 204 bottom

Hammersmith and Fulham Archives and Local History Collection: 49; 67 top; 67 bottom; 103; 149; 174

Hampstead Garden Suburb Archives: 108

Hulton Deutsch Collection: Front jacket; back jacket; 2-3; 22; 23; 24; 28; 32; 40; 47; 50; 50-51; 53; 57; 58; 59; 60; (*Rischgitz*); 65; 66; 68; 69; 71; 72-3; 75; 85 bottom; 94; 102; 105; 115; 116; 124; 126; 127 top; 129; 130-131; 142 bottom; 143; 144; 145 bottom; 146 (*Beresford*); 151; 153 bottom (*Beresford*); 158; 159; 160; 164; 169; 171 bottom; 178 top; 178 bottom; 180; 182; 186; 188; 192 (*Downey*); 193; 195; 197; 202; 203; 204 top

Imperial War Museum: 205

Peter Jackson Collection: 33; 80; 177

Lancelyn Green Collection: 153 top (*E.O. Hoppê*)

London Transport Museum: 81

The Raymond Mander and Joe Mitchenson Theatre Collection: 122 (*Bassano*); 132 left and right; 133 left and right (*W & D Downey*)

The Mansell Collection Ltd: 45 left

Mary Evans Picture Library: 93; 145 top; 171 top; 181; 185 bottom

Mirror Syndication International: 25 top; 79

Museum in Docklands, PLA Collection: 11; 31; 36-7; 38 bottom; 39

Museum of London: 184; 185 top

NMPFT/Science & Society Picture Library: 20; 21; 141 right; 154-5

National Motor Museum, Beaulieu: 12; 199 top

National Portrait Gallery: 14 (Chancellor of Dublin); 35 top right; (*F.G. Hodsoll*); 55 (*W & D Downey*); 64 left (*Van de Weyde*); 64 right (*Alice Hughes*); 70 (*Bassano*); 142 top (*Mrs Albert Broom*); 147 (*F.G. Hodsoll*); 152 (*Filson Young*)

The Press Association: 38 top; 41; 56; 110; 135; 136-7; 176; 183; 196

© RCHME Crown Copyright: 26; 34; 35 bottom left; 88 top; 89; 98; 99; 101; 113; 134; 78 (*Bedford Lemere* and following pictures): 95; 96; 97; 100; 106; 112; 157; 201-2

The Royal Archives © Her Majesty Queen Elizabeth II: 17; 18; 52; 54

The Royal Photographic Society: 8 (*Paul Martin*); 62-3 (*Horace Nicholls* and following pictures): 74; 104; 111

The Salvation Army International Heritage Centre: 167; 172; 175

Sean Sexton: 114

Sotheby's: 150 (*Alvin Langdon Coburn*)

Southampton City Heritage Services - Burrough Hill Collection: 25

By courtesy of the Board of Trustees of the Victoria & Albert Museum: 107; 42 (*Lafayette* and following pictures): 45 right; 46; 61; 128

Visual Arts Library: 140

Whitechapel Art Gallery: 148

Wigmore Hall: 118

Index

Numbers in italics refer to photgraphs

actor-managers 118
Admiralty Arch 189, *200*
Ainley, Henry 121
Albert, King of the Belgians *193*
Albert, Prince Consort 9, 10, 15, 16, 43
Aldwych 77, *88*
Aldwych Theatre 77, *88*
Alexander, George 118
Alexandra, Queen 16, 17, *18*, *43*, 44, 47, *55*, 117, 187, *192*, *194*
Alfonso XIII, King of Spain *193*
Alice, Princess *59*
Alington, Lord and Lady *65*
American heiresses 48-9, *71*
Apollo Theatre, Shaftesbury Avenue 117
artists 10, 117, 123, *146*, *148*
Asquith, Herbert Henry 163, *177*
Asquith, Margot *64*
Australia 28-9, 30

Baden-Powell, Lord: statue 33
Balfour, Arthur James 163, 188
Ballets Russes 123, *123*
balloon races *68*
balls 47-8, *64*, *65*
Barkers, Kensington High Street *97*
Barnett, Dame Henrietta 81-2
Barnett, Rev. Samuel *148*
Barrie, James *150*, *151*
bathing *173*
Beak Street: Robinson and Cleaver 78, *112*
Bechstein Hall, later Wigmore Hall *118*
Bedford College, Regent's Park *170*
Beerbohm, Max *152*, *185*
Belle of New York, The 117, *133*
Bennett, Arnold 32; *Anna of the Five Towns* 123
Bentley, E. C.: *Trent's Last Case* 123
Bernhardt, Sarah 121, *128*
Bioscope cinema, Victoria 121
Bishop's Park, Fulham *49*
Blackfriars Bridge Road *40*
Blériot, Louis *24*
Boat Race, the *142*
Boer War 15, *22*, 30, 32-3, *43*, *53*, 161, *202*
Bolm, Adolph: in *The Firebird* 123
Booth, Charles 161
Booth, William 161
Boundary Street Estate, Shoreditch 82, *109*
Bourne Estate, Clerkenwell Road *83*
Bow Street Police Court *25*
Brewer, H. W. 10
Bright, John: quoted 161
British Museum: Edward VII Galleries 80
Brock, Thomas 189
Buchan, John: *Prester John* 123
Buckingham Palace 43, *59*, 161, 187, 189, *198*; Edward VII's coffin 187, *187*; Garden Party *57*
Burnet, John 81; British Museum 80
Burns, John *183*
Burroughs, Edgar Rice: *Tarzan of the Apes* 123
Butler, Samuel: *The Way of All Flesh* 123
Butt, Alfred 117

Campbell-Bannerman, Sir Henry 165
Carnegie, Andrew 9, 121, *149*
cartes-de-visite 16, 17, *133*
Chamberlain, Joseph 29, *35*
Chambers, Mrs Lambert *145*

Charing Cross Hospital *205*
charity organisations 161, *162*
Chekhov, Anton 119
Chesterton, G. K.: *The Man Who Was Thursday* 123
Chinese immigrants 162, *178*
Churchill, Lady (Jennie Jerome) 49
Churchill, Lord Randolph 49
Churchill, Winston 10, 13, 32, 44, 49, 163, 164, 165, *177*, *181*, *188*, 190
cinemas 117, 121, *156*
Cinematograph Theatre, Edgware Road *156*
City Imperial Volunteers 32
City of London 77
Clapham: 'the capital of Suburbia' 82
Coliseum, St Martin's Lane 121, 123, *128*, *132*, 190
Colonial Office 27-9, *34*, *135*
concert halls 117, *118*, *124*
Conrad, Joseph: *Lord Jim* 123; *Secret Agent* 12
Covent Garden *65*, *114*; Theatre 123, *123*
Crane, Stephen *148*
Craven, Countess of (Cornelia Martin) 49
cricket at Lord's 48, *63*
Crippen, Dr Hawley Harvey *25*
Crisp Street market, Poplar *115*
Crossley, T. W. H.: *The Suburbans* 82
Crystal Palace, Sydenham *138*, *139*; football *143*
Curzon of Kedleston, Lord and Lady *64*, *88*

daguerreotypes 15
Daily Bioscope, Bishopsgate 121
Daily Mail 24
Daily Mirror 192
dances *136*; *see also* balls
Davison, Emily 165
debutantes 48, *60*, 165
Decline and Fall of the British Empire, The 29
department stores 80-81, *92*, *93*, *94*, *96*, *97*, *112*
Deptford Town Hall *101*
Devonshire, Duchess of *88*; Ball (1897) 47-8, *64*
Diaghilev, Sergei: Ballets Russes 123, *123*
Dickens and Jones *92*
Docks *see* London Docks
Dollar Princess, The 48
domes 78, *112*, *113*
Doyle, Arthur Conan 123, *152*
Drummond, Flora *185*
Dudley Ward, Eugenie, Fanny, Eveline *61*
Dufferin, Marchioness of (Florence Davis) 49

East, Sir Alfred *146*
East End *115*, 161, 162, *168*, *169*, *173*, *178*, *181*
Edgware Road: Cinematograph Theatre *156*
education 163, *170*
Edward VII: as Prince of Wales 9, 15, *15*, 16, 17, *18*, 44, *45*, 47, *47*, *64*, 82, *89*; coronation *17*, *49*, *50*, *53*, *54*, *55*, *125*, *131*; as King 12, 15, *43*, 43-4, 48, *50*, *67*, *85*, 117, *126*, *131*, 187-8, 189; death 123, 187, *187*, *192*; funeral 187, 188, *193*, *194*
Edwardes, George 117; *The Girl on Film* *104*
Edwards, John Passmore *149*
Egyptian Hall, Piccadilly *119*
Elgar, Sir Edward 10, *125*
Empire Theatre, Leicester Square 121, *131*
Entente Cordiale 187, 188

Fallières, President Armand *67*
'farthing breakfasts' *173*
Faussett, Captain Bryan: wedding (1907) *61*
Fehr, H. C. *98*

Ferdinand, King of Bulgaria *193*
films 117, *119*; studios 121
Football League *143*
Forbes-Robertson, Johnston 118; *Hamlet* (film) 121
Foreign Office 27; Grand Staircase *27*
Forster, E. M.: *Howards End* 123
Frampton, Sir George: Peter Pan (statue) *151*
Franco-British Exhibition (1908) *66*, *67*
Frederick VIII, King of Denmark *193*
Friern secondary school *170*
Fry, Roger 123
Fulham: Bishop's Park *49*; public library *149*; Union Infirmary *174*

Gaelic League 162
Gaiety Theatre, The Strand 77, *104*, 117
Galsworthy, John 12, 118, 123, *150*
Gandhi, Mahatma 33; statue 33
George I, King of the Hellenes *193*
George V: as Prince of Wales 15, *87*; coronation 15, *197*; as King 13, 121, 123, 165, 188, *188*, 189, *193*; and World War I 189-90, 191
German Embassy, 9 Carlton House Terrace *204*
German immigrants 162
Gibson, James: Middlesex Guildhall 79, *98*
Globe (now Gielgud) Theatre 117
Golders Green Station 81
Gordon, General Charles: statue *33*
Gorky, Maksim 163
Gosse, Edmund: *Father and Son* 123
Grafton Galleries: 1911 Exhibition 117, 123
Granville Barker, Harley 118, *150*
Grey, Sir Edward: quoted 190

Haakon VII, King of Norway *193*
Hammersmith 81, *103*
Hammerstein, Oscar 77
Hampstead Garden Suburb 81-2, *108*
Hardie, (James) Keir 161, *202*
Harrods 81, *94*
hats, women's *61*, 117
Haymarket Theatre *117*
Hello Rag-Time! 117, *133*, 190
Henry of Prussia, Prince 189
His Majesty's Theatre 118
Hobhouse, L. T. 82-3
hospitals *174*, *205*
Hotel Cecil, The Strand *88*
House of Commons *54*
Hurlingham: balloon races *68*
Hyde Park 48, *73*, *75*

Ibsen, Henrik 119
immigrants 161-2, *178*
India Office 27, *28*, 29, *29*
Irish immigrants 162
Irving, Henry 118, *129*
Italian immigrants *178*

James, Henry: quoted 9, 44, 48
Jay, Elizabeth *126*
Jewish immigrants *169*
John, Augustus *146*

Karsavina, Tamara 123, *123*
Keppel, Alice 44, 47, *47*, 187
King Street, Hammersmith *103*
Kingsway 15, 77, *78*, *84*, *85*
Kipling, Rudyard 10; *Kim* 123
Kitchener, Lord *53*, 190; statue 33

Kodak: No. 1 box camera *18*; shop *21*
Kyasht, Lydia 123

'labour exchanges' 163
Labour Party 161, *181*
Langtry, Lillie 44, *45*
Lawrence, D. H.: *Sons and Lovers* 123
Leicester Square: Empire Theatre 121, *131*
le Neve, Ethel *25*
Lenin, V. I. 163, 164
Le Queux, William: *Spies of the Kaiser* 12-13
Levey, Ethel *133*
Liberty's, Regent Street *112*
libraries, public (free) 121, 123, *149*, 162
Limehouse 161, 162
Litvinov, Maksim 163
Lloyd, Marie 117, 121, *132*
Lloyd George, David 10, 49, 163, 165, *177*, *185*
London Bridge *frontis.*, *155*
London County Council (LCC) 161; housing estates
    82, *82*, *83*, *109*; Kingsway project 77-8
London Day by Day (newsreel) 121
London Docks 30, *30*; Millwall *36*; Royal Victoria
    38; St Katharine's *38*; West India *39*
London Film Company 121
London Hippodrome 117, *133*
London Opera House 77, *78*, 117
London University *170*
London Zoo *41*
Lord's Cricket Ground 48, *63*
Loubet, President Emile 188
Louis of Battenburg, Prince 190
Louise, Princess 17
Luxemburg, Rosa 163
Lyceum Theatre *129*

MacDonald, (James) Ramsay 161
Mall, The 15, 189, *200*
Manuel of Portugal, King *193*
markets *114*, *115*
Marlborough, Duchess of 48, 49
Marlborough, Duchess of (Consuelo Vanderbilt) *71*
Marlborough, 8th Duke of 49
Marlborough, 9th Duke of *71*
Mary, Princess *87*
Masterman, C. F. G.: *The Condition of England* 83
maternity care *175*
Maude, Cyril 121
May, Edna *133*
Methodist Central Hall, Westminster 78
Middlesex Guildhall, Parliament Square 79, *98*
Millar, Gertie 117
Millbank Estate 82, *82*
Moss, H. E. 119
Motor Show, Olympia (1905) *126*
Mountbatten, Lord Louis 190
Mudie's Library 121, 123
music halls 117, 119, 121, *131*, *133*

National Insurance Act (1911) 163, *175*
negatives, retouching *21*
Nicolson, Harold: quoted 9
Nijinsky, Vaslav 123
Northcliffe, Lord *24*
Northumberland Avenue: hotels *89*
Novikoff, Laurent *135*

Old Bailey: Central Criminal Court 79
Old Ford Picture Palace *156*
Olympia: Motor Show (1905) *126*
Olympic Games (1908) *23*
Orczy, Baroness: *The Scarlet Pimpernel* 123

Paddington Station *159*
Pall Mall 80, *100*

Pankhurst, Christabel *185*
Pankhurst, Emmeline 165, *185*
Parliament Square: Middlesex Guildhall 79, *98*
Pavlova, Anna *135*
Paxton, Sir Joseph: Crystal Palace *138*
Pearly Kings and Queens *140*
pensions, old age 163, 188
Peter Pan (statue) *151*
Peter Robinson (department store) *93*
photo-journalism 17
Piccadilly: Egyptian Hall *119*; Ritz Hotel 80, *80*
Piccadilly Circus 78, *79*
Pichon, Stephen, French Foreign Minister 187
Pietri, Dorando *23*
Polish immigrants 162
Ponsonby, Sir Frederick 44, 187
Pontings, Kensington High Street *94*
Pool of London *10*
Poplar 115, *168*, *169*
Port of London 30
Portland, Duke of *88*
Post-Impressionist Exhibition (1911) 123
poverty 161-2, *162*, 163, *167*, *168*

Queen's Hall, Langham Place 117, *124*
Queen's Theatre, Shaftesbury Avenue 117

Regent Street 77, 78, *90*, *92*, *93*, *102*, *112*, 161
Regent Theatre, Upper Regent Street 118
Richardson, Mary 165
Ritz Hotel, Piccadilly 80, *80*
Roberts, Lord: statue 33
Robey, George 117, 119, *132*
Robinson and Cleaver, Beak Street 78, *112*
Rolfe, Frederick: on Westminster Cathedral *110*
Roosevelt, President Theodore 187
Rose, Donald *202*
Rothenstein, John: on Augustus John *146*
Rothschild, Lord 32
Royal Automobile Club, Pall Mall 80, *100*
Royal Court Theatre, Sloane Square 118-19, *150*
Royal Holloway College, Egham, Surrey *170*
Royal Society of Medicine, Wimpole St. *35*
Russell and Sons (photographers) 17
Russian Ballet 123; *The Firebird* 123
Russians and Russian immigrants 162, 163-4, *178*
Rutland, Duchess of *88*

St James's Park *198*
St Martin-in-the-Fields *53*
St Paul's Cathedral *18*, *22*
Sargent, John Singer 10
Scott, Sir George Gilbert Scott 27, *28*
Scottish community 163
Season, The 47, 48, *73*; *see also* debutantes
Selfridges, Oxford Street 80-81, *96*
Seven Dials 161
Shaftesbury Avenue 117
Shakespeare, William: *Hamlet* 121, *128*; *A Midsummer
    Night's Dream* 118; *Romeo and Juliet* 121
Shaw, (George) Bernard 10, 118, *150*; *John Bull's
    Other Island* 118-19; *Press Cuttings* 119
Shaw, Norman: Swan and Edgar's 78, *79*
Shoreditch: Boundary Street Estate 82, *109*
Sidney Street, Siege of (1910) 164, *177*
sport *23*, *143*, *144*, *145*, 190; *see also* Boat Race
Stalin, Joseph 163
Stamfordham, Lord 191
stations, railway and underground *24*, 81, *159*
statues: Boer War 33, *33*; Anna Pavlova *135*; Peter
    Pan *151*; Victoria 189, *198*
Stephen, Sir Leslie *152*
Stepney 161, 162, *167*, *173*, *178*
Stoll, Oswald 119, 121, 123, *128*, *132*

Strand 77, *88*, *104*, 117
Strand Theatre 77, *88*
strikes 161, 163, 164, *164*, *182*
suburbia 81-3
Suffragette movement *161*, 164-5, *184*, *185*, 188
Swan and Edgar's, Piccadilly Circus 78, *79*

Tankerville, Countess of (Leonora van Marter) 49
tea dances (*thés dansants*) 117, *136*
Tearle, Godfrey: *Romeo and Juliet* (film) 121
Terry, Ellen *129*
Thames, River *10*, *142*, *155*; *see also* London Docks
Thames Ironworks Yard 190, *191*
theatres 77, *117*, 117-19, 121, *129*, *131*, *150*
Thunderer, H.M.S. 190, *191*
Tillett, Ben *182*
Titanic 25
Tottenham Court Road: Y.M.C.A. *113*
Townsend, Charles: Whitechapel Art Gallery *148*
trade unions 161, 163
Trafalgar Square *9*, *25*, 189, *202*
traffic 15, 77, *77*, *90*, *104*
trams *84*, *85*, *87*
Transport Strike (1912) *164*
Tree, Henry Beerbohm 118
Trotsky, Lev 163

Underground railway 81, *81*, 83
unemployment 161, 163, *181*

variety theatre 121
Vaughan, Cardinal Herbert 79
Victoria, Princess *18*
Victoria, Queen 9, 15, *15*, 16, 44, 47, 79; Diamond
    Jubilee 16, *18*, 30, *32*; death 43, 187
Victoria and Albert Museum 79-80, *106*
Victoria Memorial 189, *198*
Victoria Palace Theatre 117, *135*
Victoria Station *24*

Waldorf Hotel, Aldwych 77, *78*
Wallace, Edgar: *Sanders of the River* 123
War Office (1906) *53*, 79
Warwick, Countess of (Daisy Brooke) 44, *47*, *88*
Waterloo Station *159*
Webb, Sir Aston 79-80, *106*, 189
Webb, Beatrice and Sidney 163
We-hai-wei 28
Wells, H. G. 12, 30; *The Invisible Man* 123
Welsh community 162-3
Westminster Abbey 79; Coronation 16, *50*
Westminster Bridge *12*
Westminster Cathedral 79, *110*
Westminster School *170*
Westmorland, Countess of *64*
Whitechapel *148*, 161
Whitechapel Art Gallery *148*
White City *66*, *67*
Whitehall 27, *53*, 79
White Star Lane office *25*
Wigmore Hall *118*
Wilde, Oscar: quoted 48
William II, Kaiser 189-90, *193*, *194*
Wimbledon Tennis Championships *144*, *145*
Wolseley, Field Marshal Lord: statue 33
Wood, Henry *124*; Promenade Concerts 117
Woolf, Virginia *152*
World War I 164-5, 188, 189-91, *202*, *204*, *205*
Wyatt, Matthew Digby 27
Wyllie, W. L. 10
Wyndham, Charles 118

Y.M.C.A., Tottenham Court Road *113*

zebras *40*